FROM MAKING A LIVING TO HAVING A LIFE

A Book for The Working Challenged™

Gloria Dunn

VIOLIN PUBLISHING COMPANY
FAIRFAX, CALIFORNIA

Published by: Violin Publishing Company, California

The author is grateful for permission to reprint the following copyrighted material and uses the words below as requested by each author's representative to signify this permission.

Words from *The Prophet* by Khalil Gibran are used by permission from the The National Committee of Gibran, 1951, © all rights reserved.

From THE PROPHET by Kahlil Gibran Copyright 1923 by Kahlil Gibran and renewed 1951 by Administrators C T A of Kahlil Gibran Estate and Mary G. Gibran. Reprinted by permission of Alfred A Knopf Inc.

From There's a Hole in My Sidewalk, © Portia Nelson, 1993, "Autobiography in Five Short Chapters," Beyond Words Publishing Inc. 800-284-9673

Publisher's Cataloging-in-Publication
(Provided by Quality Books Inc.)

Dunn, Gloria
    From making a living to have a life : a book for
the working challenged / Gloria Dunn ; [editor: Amanita
Rosenbush ; illustrator : Trina Swerdlow ; book designer :
Todd Crawshaw] — 1st ed.
    p. cm.
    Includes bibliographical references and index.
    LCCN: 97-80933
    ISBN: 0-9660867-5-9

    1. Career changes. 2. Career development. 3. Job
stress. 4. Burn out (Psychology). 5. Job satisfaction.
I. Rosenbush, Amanita II. Swerdlow, Trina. III.
Crawshaw, Todd IV. Title.

HF5384.D86 1999   650.14
                  QBI98-1525

I dedicate this book to
the two most important men in my life:

Donald Violin, my fiancé,
who lights up my life,

and Mark Van Brooks, my brother,
who made sure I still have one.

Acknowledgments

I feel most fortunate for the talented and supportive people in my life who have helped me make this book possible. Although the book carries my message and my mission, this book would not exist if it weren't for the loving and professional support of my sweetheart and husband-to-be, Donald Violin, who believes in me, contributes daily to my joy, and has willingly done a million things to support my putting this book out in the world; the talent and genius of my editor, Amanita Rosenbush, who helped me expand, organize and express my ideas on paper; the phenomenal creativity of Todd Crawshaw, who designed the book's exquisite cover and reader-friendly interior format; and the extraordinary artistic ability of Trina Swerdlow, who illustrated the clever and unique line drawings in the book and designed The Working Challenged™ logo. I also have many good people to thank for reading and commenting on my chapters, giving me advice, and recommending people to interview and work with. My deep gratitude to Sue Aikin, Ken Braly, Rita Derbas, Bobbi Fischer, Louise Lang, Tami Morris, Dee Pearce and Trina Swerdlow, and others whose conversations sparked ideas and contributed to this effort. I also greatly appreciate the many people who shared their stories, which helped make the copy come alive. I have changed their names and some facts in their stories to protect their privacy.

I continue to be grateful for the diversity of talents that each person offers to the world. When you have an idea and a passion to achieve something, you can accomplish it when you draw on the expertise, unique talents, and gifts of others.

From the deepest place within me, I thank you all.

"And what is it to work with love?
It is to weave the cloth with threads drawn
from your heart, even as if your beloved
were to wear that cloth.
It is to build a house with affection,
even as if your beloved
were to dwell in that house.
It is to sow seeds with tenderness
and reap the harvest with joy,
even as if your beloved were
to eat the fruit.
It is to charge all things you fashion
with a breath of your own spirit,
And to know that all the blessed dead
are standing about you and watching."
— Kahlil Gibran

"[The job] is about a search, too,
for daily meaning as well as daily bread,
for recognition as well as cash,
for astonishment rather than torpor;
in short, for a sort of life rather than
a Monday through Friday sort of dying.
Perhaps immortality, too, is part of the quest."
— Studs Terkel

CONTENTS

THE DAY I RAN AWAY FROM HOME

"However long the dream is dreamt
However long the time is spent
Whatever you are meant to do
Move toward it, and it will come to you."
— *The Author*

Have you ever wanted to run away from home? From your job? I did both.

It happened at a point when my life was not working, my job was stressful and my morale was low. I was working as a marketing director for a start-up company with people who had an ineffective management style. Their motto, unfortunately, was, "I'd rather fight than switch," which meant they clung stubbornly to ways that were unproductive and ultimately frustrating for the staff. So a typical day at work was characterized by resentment, arguments, and strife.

When I was first hired to work there, I thought I had found a job that was the opportunity of a lifetime. It promised to combine all my expertise and educational skills. I was excited beyond belief at my good fortune.

As a brand new employee, I was naturally enthusiastic. On the second day there, I met with my boss to share my ideas about promoting his business. I suggested a half dozen ways for the company to attract customers, and my boss asked me to come up with a written proposal. I found the project so stimulating that I worked all weekend on it. First thing Monday morning I brought it in, knowing from all my background and expertise that these ideas were winners.

After all, it was my know-how that, in the past, had helped the companies I worked for succeed and won me professional awards as well.

As I walked into my boss's office, he looked up solemnly. It wasn't a good sign, but perhaps he hadn't had his coffee yet. I handed him my proposal. He read it for several minutes while I stood waiting for his go-ahead to launch my grand campaign. When he finished, he set the pages on his desk and said in a flat voice, "There is no money in the budget for this kind of thing. We cannot implement this promotion. You'll have to think of something else."

I stood there dumbfounded, as stunned as if I had been slapped across the face. "I don't believe this," I said to myself. "Why didn't he tell me this before I went through all that work? And why did he even hire me in the first place if he can't afford my ideas?" *Deflation Number One.*

Several days passed. I used the time to study the marketplace and look for other promotional avenues. Again I went in to see my boss and present my suggestions. His business was in an upscale neighborhood, and he needed to get the word out in a stylish way if he wanted to make a good impression. I recommended sending out high-quality brochures. I also suggested following that up by holding an event on-site and inviting prospective customers to come and see the services and staff for themselves. Once again, my boss watched me silently and answered atonally, "Send out inexpensive flyers instead and forget about the event." *Deflation Number Two.*

It took my boss several months to realize that his cheap methods weren't working. Finally, he gave in to my original proposal. Within six weeks of implementing it, hundreds of new customers showed up. Instead of rewarding me, however, he seem disgruntled that I had been right and sucked the value out of my efforts by saying, "We don't need any more of that upscale promotional stuff." After that, the tasks he gave me were of lower and lower quality. *Deflation Number Three.*

The vice-president of the company, seeing how disconsolate I was, offered me some unwelcomed advice. "If you want something in this place, you have to fight for it." The only problem was, I hadn't come there to fight. I had come to work.

There was a time in my life when I would have stayed in a job like that a little longer and tried to make it work out, but something told me to abandon this yo-yo existence. I no longer wished to allow my creativity to be leached, my competence to be overlooked, my skills to be under-used, or my personal being to be violated. I quit one Friday afternoon, and I was not surprised when, six months later, the business failed.

Many employees worldwide suffer similar insults to their talents. All too often, the top management of organizations have no people skills, and they make all the classic supervisory mistakes. They misuse highly skilled employees, they refuse to apply the very ideas they are paying them to come up with, and they neglect to praise their accomplishments. The employees want to be effective, but management cuts them off at the knees.

So here I was, unemployed. At the same time, my personal life happened to be falling apart. A classic mid-life crisis was making me ask questions like: *Who am I? Why am I here? How do I put meaning into my life?* The experience at my last job had convinced me that I needed to find a whole new direction away from corporate America. But I was still living *in* America, and that meant I needed a paycheck.

Suddenly, I felt like a car that was completely out of alignment. Part of me had been indoctrinated all my life with a strong work ethic and a sense of responsibility. I was supposed to get up early and go to work every day. I was supposed to earn my keep. The other part of me, on the other hand, was more rebellious. It kept saying, "Good for you for quitting. Do everything you can to make things work out. Other than that, trust in God." I needed to rearrange my life and, in the process, not drive myself crazy with self-doubt.

The one persistent feeling that pervaded that period of time was that I had simply had enough. I knew I had to get away from it all. Not just from work, but from home and responsibilities and everything. I needed time to reflect, to get unstuck, if I was going to learn how to make my life work again. The message I kept getting from inside myself was *SIMPLIFY*. I needed a less complex, less hectic environment where life could be a little quieter. I needed to dramatically shift old patterns so that I could begin to say "I can" instead of "I can't." And most of all, I needed to regain the self-esteem I had lost at my job. If I was ever to fulfill my life's purpose, it was clear that I first needed to know *what it was*. I realized I was not the only person in the world ever to be faced with the dilemma of finding a way to take the time and find answers to these mega-questions, and still survive financially. I just needed to figure out a way to do it.

In search of escape and in want of an opportunity to find myself, I talked to my then significant other, Ben*. He was bored with his job, too, and had wanted to change professions. Like me, he was stuck, and he agreed to make a drastic change in our environment. New place, new lives.

Never before had we considered relocating, and we had absolutely no place in mind to go. One day, Ben remembered a town in the Sierra foothills that we had driven through on the way to go skiing — Sonora. It sounded as good a place as any to start. Even the word Sonora was beautiful. One winter day, we drove up to look around. The gods must have been speaking to Ben when he came up with that idea, for the evergreen trees, the fresh country air, and the deep sense

* I have changed his name to protect his privacy.

of peace convinced us immediately to look for a house to rent. It all happened in the twinkle of an eye!

It may sound a little unsound that after quitting my job so precipitously, I chose a new place to live just as quickly. It often does make sense to check out other possibilities when making a big decision, to make a pros and cons list, to sleep on it for a month. Perhaps so, but life doesn't always work out that way, and for me, the right choice was to pick up and go. I knew that prolonging the decision would not help me make a better one, but would only make me more miserable than I already was. In addition, I had some past experience to give me an extra boost. I had taken risks before in my life and they had always worked out beautifully. The results, over time, had built into me the belief that the only way to explore one's future was by trying something new.

This country, in fact, is built on that kind of thinking. Imagine the courage the Pilgrims had to muster up to climb aboard those creaky ships and sail across the Atlantic Ocean back in the seventeenth century. They might have been able to survive in England, but they would never have been happy, fulfilled, or free. And the pioneers who forged their way west in covered wagons to homestead the wild frontier were heading into dangers both known and unknown. Like all of these people, I was willing to take some risks in order to have a better life — only I was traveling in a 1982 Honda Prelude.

So there I found myself on the day before my forty-ninth birthday, in the same Sierras the pioneers had crossed a century earlier. Ben and I found a sweet little A-frame house on two and a half acres of sprawling meadow. Instantly, we both knew we were in the home we were meant to have. The ceiling had redwood beams, the living room was an open space that led into the kitchen area, and there was an old-fashioned wood-burning stove on the far wall. All around, the house was protected by a covey of trees. Even so, as Ben and I filled out the rental agreement, I was filled with concern and uncertainty and yet overcome with excitement and a sense of adventure. I wondered if in making this move, I was either being very foolish or very brave, very crazy or very sane.

We returned to the San Francisco Bay Area to put our affairs in order. Inside I was asking, "Will I be happy where I'm moving? Will I use this time in a more disciplined way to reflect and integrate what I'm learning? Am I just kidding myself, or is this the right thing to do?" On the outside, I was having the phone disconnected, having the electricity turned off, and having my mail rerouted. It was fortunate for me that during this transition, I got all the positive reinforcement I needed from my friends to keep my spirits up. They took me out for a combined birthday/bon voyage celebration and reassured me that everything was going to be all right.

Even customer service people at the utility companies were supportive. When they heard I was moving to the Sierra foothills, they lit up. "I'm jealous," one woman at the other end of the phone said. "I love it up there. My husband and I thought about buying a home in the area, but we decided we couldn't afford it." She paused. "I think we could have afforded it," she added regretfully. Others told me I was brave and gutsy to make the big move and wished they could do it, too.

This combination of responses made me realize that I was living out a dream others had thought about but never acted on. When I reflected on it, it occurred to me that one of the major reasons other people did not do what Ben and I were doing was that they were afraid that if they failed they would end up homeless, living on the streets out of a supermarket cart. I think the reason I was willing to take the risk is that finding out who I am and what I am meant to do in life has always been more important to me than security or material possessions. So perhaps it did not seem to be as big a risk to me as it would have been for some people.

When we finally moved into our new home and I got to know the neighborhood, I found that there was always some way to make an income. It wasn't enough to put a Jacuzzi in the back yard or buy a new car, but Ben and I didn't need that kind of thing to be happy. Life, as it turns out, is much simpler in the country. The fees from the public relations and foreign student exchange projects I found and the work-shops I gave, plus the income from Ben's job, were enough to pay the rent and put food on the table. In place of mone-tary wealth, I gained enormous wealth of a different kind — riches for the soul.

Imagine taking long strolls through the countryside; fill-ing your lungs with clean fresh air; letting the dog off the leash; picking yellow, purple and pink flowers from the meadow and putting them in a vase on the kitchen win-dowsill; gazing out at a 400-year old oak tree in your very own meadow. Consider what it's like to have the time to improve your tennis game, go to the Crazy Horse Saloon and dance, wander lazily through the streets of a town that has only one stoplight. All those hours were freed up for me because I now didn't have to spend them sitting in traffic at seven in the morning or meeting the unrealistic expectations of bosses who had no idea how much they were requesting. And at night in the country, Ben and I could easily enjoy an array of events or just gaze at the stars.

I also had time to be involved in the community. In line with my extroverted nature, I joined a number of service organizations where I was able to make new friends and contribute my skills for the good of the community.

When I look back on it, I can see that our decision to *"run away from home"* was one of the healthiest things we could have done. If I had spent years conducting a survey of various locations in which to live, I could not have selected a better place for myself than I had in that one twenty-four hour period on a cool winter morning. In the two years that I lived in the hills of the Sierras, I experienced the true value of community and the exquisite joys of country life, and — surprise! — I found my next career. It was there, in the laid-back timelessness of nature, that I realized that I wanted to be a professional speaker and help others realize their dreams.

I now know that the fact that my job as a marketing director made me miserable was actually a gift. Had I been comfortable there, I might be in that cubicle still, writing proposals that nobody took seriously. I would never have been pushed out into the world to explore the next phase of my life or learned any of the important lessons that I did. In short, I might never have gone from just *making a living* to *having a life*.

Not everyone needs to make a big change. Running away isn't right for everybody. This was my way, and it worked for me, but I do not advocate it as the grand cure for all troubles. However, I also do not advocate staying stuck in an environment that is filled with confusion, apathy, pain, and strife. Throughout this book, I will offer you different options for exploring your work life. I've told you what worked for me. Let's see what works for you.

CHAPTER ONE

WORK IS MORE THAN A PAYCHECK

"I think the person who takes a job in order
to live — that is to say, for the money —
has turned himself into a slave."
— *Joseph Campbell*

If I were to ask you why you work, you probably would say, "To earn money." If I asked you whether you would keep working if you had all the money you needed, you might answer, "No way!" I contend that if you loved what you did, you would do it even if the paycheck was unnecessary. This is not to negate the importance of getting paid. Besides being of enormous practical value, that check is one of the ways in which the world communicates to us that our work has worth. *Wise work*, however, is so much more than that.

Wise work involves using the whole of yourself, connecting to your inherent talents, skills, creativity, and inner wisdom. In some ways, you feel you are doing what you are born to do, and that no one can do your particular job as well as you. Working wisely means you are actualizing your own potential and that everything you produce is a natural expression of who you are. Under these conditions, it is not hard to produce excellent results as well as experience a high degree of satisfaction.

A job that does not incorporate wise work, on the other hand, produces no such satisfaction. Although you may use your brain or your back to repair cars, broker stocks, sell food, or participate in one of countless other vocations, if you are not using your essence, the end product feels impersonal. Even if you drive yourself toward excellence in a job

1

you're not meant to be doing, it is only the employer's needs that are filled, not your own.

Chad
Ever since I was a child, I dabbled in some form of business. When I was nine, I ran a lemonade stand. When I was ten, I started selling newspapers along with the lemonade. By the time I was thirteen, people could buy a glass of lemonade, their morning paper, and a bouquet of flowers all on the same street corner. And by the time I was in high school, I knew my way around well enough to help other teens start their own businesses. Today I'm a venture capitalist, and I still get a buzz out of guiding entrepreneurs and putting deals together.

Not every venture capitalist gets a buzz out of it. Some of them should be journalists or sailboat captains or teachers. Chad, though, was drawn to this work because he had a knack for what it involved — seeing opportunity, taking risks, and marshaling resources to put ideas into action. All these skills were packed into Chad's genes before he was ever born, and since then have been nurtured by life experiences.

Chad was more fortunate than most. He could have been pressured, as many are, to head in a direction that was prescribed by others instead of by himself. He might have been talked into going to medical school for example, since that's what his father did. Instead, Chad did what most people don't do — he followed the path of least resistance. Far from being the lazy way, it is the most promising direction to take. Author Robert Fritz calls it letting your "energy move where it is easiest for it to go." Chad looked at what he did well, at what talents came naturally to him, at what he actually enjoyed; and he decided to make a living by heading that way.

Many people feel that what is expected of them is to pick something to do for a living that makes a respectable income. This can force them to live a life of quiet desperation. They search endlessly for happiness in the situation they are in, yet never seem to find it. No matter how miserable they are, they are afraid to let go of what they perceive to be stability. If they do make a change, they find themselves immersed in the same problems all over again because what they changed over to was not significantly different from what they had left. My belief is that they are not following their own inner guidance, the voice inside that tells us when we are going down the wrong path.

Mel

I didn't know what to do when I got out of high school. Since I was an idealist, law school seemed like a logical choice because it represented a lofty profession. But the first job I took after graduating was anything but lofty. All I did was push paper around and worry about billable hours. I went on from that firm to work for an airline and then for a computer software company. In each case, either I chose to move on or I was downsized. Wherever I found myself, though, it wasn't the right place. I was just wandering without a plan. Finally, when I lost my job for the third time, I had a severe panic attack and began to hyperventilate because my savings account balance was hovering around zero. My wife actually had to rush me to the emergency room. As it turns out, I was fine, but that scare gave me a new appreciation for life and made me look at work in a whole different way. I realized that the one activity I had engaged in over the years that I really enjoyed was kayaking. In fact, I had met my wife, Shirley, that way. She and I decided to start our own business coordinating kayaking vacations for people in search of personal renewal. Today, I'm more stable and more happy than I've ever been.

Often circumstances that seem beyond our control — layoffs, accidents, deaths — serve us by jarring our awareness and opening our minds. If we are wise, we recognize times like these as crucial moments for making decisions. We have a choice: either we can go on doing things the way we always have and get the same results, or we can use the opportunity to take a new direction. If we are brave enough to make the necessary changes, we are rewarded quite often with rich, satisfying work and fuller lives. If we ignore the moment, pass up the opportunity, and keep going down the same road, we feel old and defeated before our time.

Just as we have bought into the myth that stability and happiness come from something outside us, we have also believed the American myth that money and material things bring joy. Advertisements, commercials, movies, and newspapers have done a good job on selling us this bill of goods. After all, if we hear and see these promises of nirvana day in and day out, they are bound to make a big impression. We begin, somewhat mindlessly, to search out this promised nirvana and put most of our time into that search. Unfortunately, satisfaction from these kinds of sources is momentary and fleeting. Acquiring things becomes addictive; needing becomes an end in itself. Pretty soon, we are going to work every day just so we can afford our *possession fix*. But the more we buy, the more we want, and so it goes.

"I had all the money and a nice job and it sucked."

— Mel

Peter

One morning when I woke up, my wife confronted me. "You're never home and if things don't change immediately, I'm getting a divorce. This time I mean it!" I knew from her voice that this time she really would follow through on her threat. I left the house and went for a long walk. "What am I doing?" I asked myself. "Time is flying by, and I'm sick and depressed half the time, and I hate my business, and I'm about to lose my wife." I remembered how things had been when I started my business, how important the new boat was, and the airplane, and the Mercedes, and the half-million dollar house. As I walked, though, I realized that none of those things had ever really brought me pleasure, just a big mortgage and hectic days. I never had time to use the boat or the plane anyway, and my wife was always in that big house by herself. But I couldn't see what was happening. I was like a chicken running around with its head cut off. I had completely lost sight of what was important to me.

Later that afternoon, I was watching a documentary on TV about the Pennsylvania Amish. They didn't have very many things, but they were happy. All of a sudden I heard myself say, "I'd like to try

5

*that." "What," my wife asked, "being happy?"
After that, I began to see that happiness comes
from the inside, not the outside. You cannot buy it;
you have to find it within yourself. From that time
on, I stopped needing a lot of money to enjoy
myself. Simpler things made me pretty content. Of
course, I was also feeling better because I wasn't
killing myself for big bucks at work. Eventually, I
quit my business, and my wife and I moved to a
small town in New England and started a horse
farm. I had liked horses ever since I was a boy, and
this place has been heaven for me.*

The Myth of Security

*"Subtract a person's material wealth and
what is left is his real wealth."*
— Malcolm S. Forbes, Sr.

In search of a paycheck, many people put the myth called
security before all the other important things in life: family,
health, relaxation, fulfillment and personal growth. Some
are so security-driven that they make themselves miserable
and are willing to accept that bottom-basement quality of
life until they retire. In the back of their minds, *that* is when
life begins, *that is* when they can finally tend to other things.

The myth is twofold. One, they believe if they stay
where they are, it will automatically mean security. Every
day, however, the world economy changes and works against
that myth. These days, working at one job for many years
does not guarantee you a gold watch and a pension, and it
may, in fact, work against you. It could be preventing you
from keeping your skill level up to the standards of the modern world. Two, they believe if they leave that "secure" job,
no good can come of it. It will be a frivolous move that will

lead them to ruin. I can tell you from the personal experience of people I interviewed for this book that this isn't so. Very often, when a person goes after his heart's desire, which in this case is wise work, the whole world conspires in numerous and mysterious ways to help him. Often, his income increases too.

Sally

At forty-seven, I consider myself an articulate and capable division manager. I work at a large financial firm, and while I do receive some of the perks you get at big companies, I hate my job. In fact, out of the five years I've worked there, I've hated it for the last three. I go to work every day with a sense of dread in my heart because I cannot stand the people I work with. Last year I missed work several times because of illness, and I was even hospitalized once with pneumonia. On the other hand, I do know my job very well, and I know what to expect every day. And in two years, I'll be vested in the retirement plan. Maybe in two years I'll be able to go out and find another job; but for now, I feel really trapped.

Oh, Sally, why do you do this to yourself? She has not taken the time to calculate the price she is paying for settling for what she has instead of going after what she wants. Subconsciously, her body is trying to tell her she is riding the horse the wrong way. That's why she keeps encountering one problem after another. What she needs to do is stop being so busy and pay attention to her deeper needs. Sadly, she isn't ready to listen to them yet. Does this sound familiar? Whenever I have gently broached this subject with her, she freely admits that she will do anything to make sure there is money in the bank when she retires.

Unfortunately, this particular fear drives many Americans. We are afraid to outlive our income. Whole financial strategies at investment houses are geared to appeal to this mentality. I do not negate this need. I, myself, am filling the coffer for my golden years. Nobody ever wants to contemplate ending up homeless in this society. Security is a legitimate driving force in all of us, and it needs to be honored. But it cannot override every other facet of life. We cannot let fear make all our decisions for us. Life is too short to be dominated by this one thing at the expense of joy, sense of accomplishment, self-expression, and pride in oneself.

The Revolution for Meaning

As a society, we are on the brink of a new era of self-discovery as more of us search for meaningful and satisfying work, and as we realize that work is not just a paycheck but a composite of who we are in action. At the same time, many of us are attempting to balance our work with the other aspects of our lives. This is bound to be a successful merger because we will ultimately work and live from our essence — our truth.

Together, we are creating a revolution that will foster the true creative self at work, as opposed to the drone whose only purpose is to carry out someone else's game plan. It will allow us to balance our lives and encourage us to express who we are, as we produce exquisite products and offer genuinely useful services to people.

In a world where wise work became the norm instead of the exception, we would not be such slaves to a paycheck. Because of how satisfying life is in so many other ways as a result of living more creatively, we would depend less on masses of material things for happiness. In addition, we would re-find old ways of exchange to take the place of money, like bartering some of our own talents and services for those of others. There are many places in the world today where this is practiced quite successfully, and it can be practiced in an industrial society, also, with a little creativity and cooperation. I know of an interior designer, for example, who exchanged her decorating skills for her bookkeeper's know-how. Both were happy with the arrangement because they got to do what they did best, and because no money changed hands. It was just a friendly deal between two people.

As we let go of old societal dictates that measure people by how much they are able to earn and accumulate, we will no longer trade our precious lives for a paycheck. It is then we will recognize that we are our own greatest asset.

SUMMARIZED POINTS

1. *Wise work* involves using the whole of yourself, connecting to your inherent talents, skills, creativity and inner wisdom.

2. A job that does not incorporate wise work is ultimately unsatisfying.

3. Let your energy move where it is easiest for it to go.

4. Follow your own inner guidance, the voice inside that tells you when you are going down the wrong path.

5. Recognize that you have a choice either to go on doing things the way you always have and get the same results, or to take a new direction.

6. When a person goes after his heart's desire, which in this case is wise work, the whole world conspires in numerous and mysterious ways to help him.

7. A new revolution is taking place that will foster the true creative self at work.

8. You are your own greatest asset.

CHAPTER TWO

How Core Beliefs Keep Us Stuck In The Wrong Job

"... yesterday is but today's memory and
tomorrow is today's dream."
— Kahlil Gibran

If you were raised in China or Japan and I asked you why you never look me in the eyes when we speak, you probably would say that it is disrespectful. Your answer would come from a cultural belief system you were taught in childhood. Your awareness of both the belief as well as the reason for your actions is in your conscious mind — you know why you prefer no eye contact. Now, suppose you move to another country where the culture encourages eye contact. Your employer tells you it supports good work relationships and enhances customer service. Since you want to keep your job, even though you feel uncomfortable changing, you decide it won't hurt you, and it may indeed help you, to adopt this new habit. Because you are distinctly aware that it is a belief, you can take steps to change it.

On the other hand, if you are a person who was raised in a home where subtle messages were continuously being passed along instead of stated outright, you will not be aware that your position is just part of a belief system. For example, you may have believed the one that says, "Children are to be seen and not heard." Now, at the age of thirty-seven, when you are afraid to speak up at meetings, you are still adhering to an old imposed rule embedded in your unconscious mind. In this case, you are not aware that you are carrying out an old belief system, so you don't realize you can change it. What you cannot see is that your hidden beliefs are keeping you from realizing your full potential at work and in life.

We all have fundamental ideas about how we and the world should be, ideas we absorbed in childhood. These core beliefs are tucked deep down inside of us and rule our lives. That is both good news and bad news. Good, because some of these assumptions give us the ability to design a life that works. Bad, because other beliefs destroy our lives. In this chapter, we will focus on how to recognize and change the unconscious beliefs that get in the way of succeeding at work.

"There I was, walking on a busy city sidewalk, not paying attention to where I was going. All of a sudden I couldn't move. I had stepped into a pile of cement and it hardened up to my ankles. I couldn't move forward. I couldn't go back. I was stuck. Then, I woke up and thought, 'That's how it feels at work.'"

— Inga

Do you ever wonder why you feel stuck in your job? Do you think it may be time for you to find an answer to that question so you can remove the chains that bind you?

The reality we experience on a day-to-day basis can be created through our core beliefs. They seem to be implicit, something we don't question. Hidden in our unconscious mind, they influence our actions, opinions, and decisions.

Changing harmful core beliefs is one of the most worthwhile tasks we can choose for ourselves. Nothing else reaps such rich rewards nor has the capacity to change our lives so much for the better. There is an internal battle going on in us all the time where one side is struggling to solve our problems and achieve our goals, and the other side is saying, "No, don't change. Just keep up the status quo." This side thwarts every attempt to improve our lives.

We say that we want our life to be meaningful and our jobs to be fulfilling, and yet those around us can often see what we cannot — that we have a particular mind-set we will not part with. This is not hard to understand since throughout our entire lives, our belief system has been evolving into what it is today.

Our core beliefs originated in childhood. Virtually every important belief we hold began when we were young and impressionable, and those decisions, made by our child mind, dictate how we react to today's problems. The trouble is, the issues we had to deal with at age five are not the same as the ones we have to deal with at age forty-five.

In addition, the potential we have to make real changes that affect our own lives is vastly improved now. At five years old, everything we did was based on coping in a world of giants, a world where we were small and relatively helpless. Now, we can make most of our own decisions and carry them out. Yet how many people stay in jobs they hate because on some level they still believe they are helpless five-year-olds?

Helen

For thirteen years, I worked at a cosmetics counter in a large department store. I am sensitive to smells and chemicals, and here I was surrounded by them every day. Whenever some manufacturer came out with a new perfume scent, I dreaded it because I knew it would mean salesgirls out in the aisles spraying customers as they came in, which only added to what was already in the environment. As bad as it got, it never occurred to me to leave. I had gotten the job straight out of high school, and at the time I was grateful for it. Friends and family would gently suggest that I at least work in another department, but whenever I brought it up to management, they said they needed me where I was.

One day, the parent company closed our store to open another one in a suburb where it would be more profitable. They gave us no warning at all. There had been rumors in the air, but no one from upstairs was saying anything, so we assumed the rumors were unfounded. Then, one Friday, we all came into work at the same time as usual, and we were notified that we would be quitting two hours early and that it was our last day. I went home feeling completely confused and helpless. Somebody I had never even met had turned my life upside down, and there was nothing I could do about it. I did have some money saved, and my rent was pretty low, so fortunately I didn't have to go out right away and grab a job at a fast food place. Several people, in fact, urged me to take my time, now that I was free — their word — to find a job that literally didn't make me sick. I realized that I had picked up a lot of skills as a salesperson while I had worked at the department store, and that if I could sell one thing, I could sell another. Through several tips, I heard about a job at a radio station selling time to advertisers. I had never thought of selling time before, but I figured if peo-ple bought it, I could sell it.

Within three months, my salary had doubled, and I loved the sense of power I felt when I brought in a new account. The funny thing was that I had never felt more helpless in my life than when I was sent home that dark Friday without a job. Yet that's what it took for me to find out that I was anything but helpless. With all that time on my hands, I reflected on my life and how I was always falling into things and then not mustering up the courage and the will to get out when it clearly wasn't work-ing. Finding this new job and being successful has made me feel really empowered.

Like millions of others, Helen's life had quietly grown into a crisis because she let things get worse and worse and didn't know she could do something about it. When Helen was a small child, it had worked for her to go along with the program and do the best she could with what life handed her. She had no choice. At some point, though, she passed that line into adulthood, and then she *did* have a choice.

Once she took charge of her life, she came into her own power and felt like a whole new person with a huge range of choices. When Helen was programmed in childhood that to go along was to get along, she was naive and impressionable and had no perspective about the world, people, or life. At that time, like little sponges, we all soaked up the attitudes of society, and of parents, teachers, and siblings. As we grew, friends, television, movies, and other outside forces also influenced us, but the real hardcore beliefs had already been formed. Most of us have not ever really questioned these beliefs. We have gotten through life with *whatever worked before,* and trauma or painful experiences have only caused us to hold on to them even more tightly. In turn, of course, this has simply reinforced our fragility and sense of limitation. We cannot imagine using new tools. The old ones, as inadequate as they may be sometimes, seem to be all we have access to.

As adults, we still act on old impressions and beliefs, even though they are often unconscious and unexamined. We do not need to throw the baby out with the bath water, however. Some early principles guide us well and are good to keep. But others, like Helen's belief that being passive was her only option, need to be eliminated because they are destructive to personal growth and happiness. If you want to take charge of your life, you need to become aware of what runs you and make sure it will support you in achieving your goals.

Why couldn't Helen see what those around her could — that she didn't actually have to stay stuck behind a cosmetics counter wheezing all day? It's easy to think, "Oh, I would never do that. I would have been out of there in a week." Certainly we would like to believe that about ourselves, but look at your own situation. Are you working someplace that has long ceased to make you happy? Has your job been stale for years, but you just hold on to it? As I said earlier, core beliefs are not so easy to spot. Helen had to get laid off to be shaken into taking a good look at herself. A core belief like hers is like a brick wall in the mind. When you see a wall, you automatically believe that you have to stop in front of

it. The conviction is so implicit that you don't even reach out to touch it to see if you can put your hand through it. It looks like a wall, and walls are solid, which means you can't walk through them, so you have to stop, right? In truth, the walls in your mind are just very convincing images that are telling you, "You can't go any further than this." The only way to find out whether it is really true or not is to test it. Try going *through* the wall and see what happens.

Often, what people find is that the walls are nothing but imaginary barriers keeping them from their heart's desire and from success. I know a woman who is a wonderful artist. Yet she cannot accept the fact that her paintings are beautiful and worthy of being purchased even though she has won awards for them. Whenever she comes close to achieving a higher level of distinction in her career, she cripples her chances by overworking her paintings in an effort to make them *more acceptable* and by missing deadlines for shows. Her father had been a highly driven executive and didn't believe much in the *artistic* life. He told her she would never amount to anything if she persisted in painting watercolors, and those words sank in. Today, she undermines herself by underpricing her work and getting it in late. Until she identifies and changes her core beliefs, she will believe her father's words, and she will continue to be a *struggling* artist.

Now is the time for us, as adults, to become the author of our own rules, to explore ourselves and determine whose principles we will live by. By the time we reach the age of consent, there ought to be principles we have consciously picked for ourselves. We no longer reside under our parents' roofs, and to live up to our true potential in life, we should not be playing by their rules. As adults, it is up to us to determine the course of our lives.

I, too, had to learn to break down a few brick walls. While one of them had to do with work, the other was more about knowing when *not* to work.

The Author
   One summer, my children's father invited them to spend several weeks with him back East. Until then, as a single parent, I had been totally responsible for them on weekdays, weekends, and vacations. For the next six weeks, however, I was free to

be responsible for no one but myself in my spare time. For a while, everything went well. I went dancing and water skiing and played tennis. I met friends for dinner, went to parties.

For Labor Day, my last free weekend without the children, I had a big water skiing trip planned with friends. Yet on the Saturday of that weekend, instead of finding myself ripping along behind a speedboat, I was sitting at a desk in front of my typewriter trying to write copy. At that time, I was a public relations specialist, and I had a magazine to produce. When my fingers went to type, though, no words would come. Ideas refused to present themselves. After some frustration, I decided I must be tired, and I went home. No water skiing, but no work either.

On Sunday, I came in again and sat grimly before my typewriter. Now, in addition to being creatively blocked, I was beginning to feel some sort of pain throughout my body, and I didn't understand it. Believing I was physically ill, once again I went home.

Determined to get the copy written, I came in again on Labor Day. So far, I had accomplished nothing. The longer I stayed at my desk, the more intense my pain grew. By noon, I was scared. It so happened that I worked in a hospital, and my office was down the hall from the Psychiatric Department. I began to wonder if I was going crazy, so I called one of the therapists from the department who told me to come into to see him the next day.

When Tuesday morning came, the therapist suggested I lie on the couch and relax. Shortly after I lay down, I popped up and said, "I don't want to relax, I want to talk." So he said, "Talk!" Within our hour visit we discovered that when I was a child my mother used to say things like, "You played this morning, why do you need to go to the movie this afternoon? You already had fun today."

I bought into her belief that people shouldn't have too much fun, and that because I had had fun other days that summer, I had reached my acceptable limit. I think this principle was part of my mother's serious Eastern European background. Whatever the reason, I took the idea of hard work and no play very seriously.

The truth was that I hadn't needed to spend any of my last free weekend working on the magazine. The deadline was far enough away to get the work finished in a four-day week. But in those few weeks of carefree summer, I had been growing unconsciously guilty about having too much fun. To punish myself, I ruined my Labor Day weekend by denying myself the opportunity to go water skiing with my friends.

As I talked it out with the therapist, something inside me knew it was time to outgrow this faulty core belief that had belonged to my mother and not me. After this grand discovery of secret guilt, which I learned was the cause of my emotional pain, the therapist told me, "You need to learn to have more fun. And if you can't take it all at once, take it s-l-o-w-l-y."

Someone once said that guilt is the gift that keeps on giving. In the past, it was freely passed on from one generation to the next. People really believed in guilt. Today, psychologists tell us it is highly unnecessary, that there are better ways to get ourselves to accept our responsibilities. We now know that guilt does far more harm than good. It has a toxic flavor to it, and while it may sometimes get results, the price in the long run is too high to pay. The healthy way to move ourselves forward is by consciously understanding what blocks us from doing what is necessary. What works is knowing ourselves as thoroughly as possible, realizing compassionately that we all make mistakes, forgiving our failures as part of the game of life, and taking all setbacks in stride as an important step in finding ultimate success. And finally, learning our lessons and using their teachings to move forward. By shedding my guilt, I have enriched my life. I can now see that play is good for me; I savor its pleasures. Amusement fills a human need and balances the serious side of life.

What Are Some of Your Core Beliefs?

Have you ever taken the time to examine your core beliefs? Do you live by your own rules or ones that were planted in you?

Pamela

My father had a strong voice and a heavy hand. I grew up with the belief that if someone raised their voice, I was going to be beaten. One day at work, my boss was irritated about what he said was a "screw-up of monumental proportions" and was ranting and raving at everyone. I was so afraid, I ran home with a fierce headache.

Then I worried all day about when I should return to work. It took years for me to learn that I was creating my own fears.

Here are some questions to ask yourself to see if you have hidden beliefs about yourself or the world that are holding you back.

- Do you think you deserve the success you have already achieved?

- Do you believe you're meant to be a success in this life?

- Do you believe you should be seen and not heard, that what you think isn't really important to anyone else?

- Do you deserve to be happy?

- When you are in a group, do you feel you belong there as much as everyone else does?

- Have you been told that work is not supposed to be fun?

- Is it your view of the world that there is enough to go around?

- When you are talking about the subject of your expertise, if your audience could see into your mind, would they see someone who feels competent or someone who thinks she is bluffing?

- Do you feel guilty when you say no to people, even if the request is out of line?

- If you stand up for yourself to others, are you afraid you'll be an outcast?

- If you leave a position of security, do you think you'll end up without a roof over your head?

What You Can Do to Change Your Core Beliefs?

The first step in changing our core beliefs is awareness. We need to see clearly all the things we accept as fact, review whether they're really accurate, and then decipher how they are manifested in our lives. Does the belief have a healthy or an unhealthy effect? Is it working toward our goals or against them? This means we have to become acutely conscious of what our patterns are, why we persist in following courses of action that never seem to give us what we want, and what the outcomes to our decisions are. Only then do we have the information we need to effect intelligent change. By following the process below, you will learn how to recognize and change the beliefs that have blocked you from leaving work you hate and finding work you love.

Step One: Observe

Creating a Self-Portrait — an Exercise in Awareness

For one week, you will be both observer and subject. From the time you get to work in the morning until you get home at night, observe yourself in various situations at your job. It's easy to lose an observation as soon as you make it, so carry a small notebook and keep careful notes about your subject. As you record it, see if you can label the nature of the observation. For example, *How I deal with conflict,* or *How I handle a crisis.* Pick a normal week in which to do this exercise, one in which work is fairly typical of the rest of the year, so that you get an accurate snapshot of yourself in daily life. There should be three parts to your observation: a) the event itself (i.e., whatever is happening); b) your internal response to the event (i.e., how you feel); and c) your external response to the event (i.e., what you do).

Below are twelve examples of the kinds of issues and situations that commonly come up in the workplace.

1. How you deal with conflict.

There is a woman at the desk next to yours who never has enough to do, and you have more than your fair share. With her available time, she is supposed to take on some of your work load. Instead, she makes personal phone calls and hangs around the water cooler complaining about the coffee. Every time she goofs off, you make a mental note of it. At lunch with your friends from the department, you point out how lucky this person is that she has so much time to make appointments with her hairdresser and talk to her sister during the work day, while you, on the other hand, have to wait until you get home. The others murmur in agreement that something isn't right.

2. How you handle criticism.

Your boss brings back some forms you filled out and points out the mistakes. You have to do them all over again. Even though he is right, you tighten up under the implied criticism. You don't like it when people tell you how to do things. You prefer to do it your own way, then find and correct mistakes yourself. You snatch the papers from his hand and mutter something as you head back to your desk.

3. How you take in compliments.

You have just finished a project that you worked very hard on. At the department meeting that day, after looking over your work, several people tell you what a thorough and admirable job you did. Four people complimenting you all at the same time embarrasses you, and you don't know what to say. To cover it up and keep from appearing too proud, you dismiss their praise and point out all the places in the project that could have been better.

4. How you respond to the demands of others.

On the first week of the month, you are always overloaded with phone calls and e-mail. It makes you anxious because you're afraid that if you don't respond to everyone immediately, they will think you're not doing your job and providing them with adequate service. Consequently, you answer every little note, memo, phone call, e-mail, and fax, even the ones you know can wait, because you hope that if you can catch up with the details your anxiety will diminish.

5. How you deal with an unruly boss.

You are unavoidably late for work because of an accident on the freeway. When you walk into the reception area, your boss scolds you in front of everyone as if you were a child.

Your face reddens, and you feel like crawling into a hole. You slink into your office and don't reappear until lunch.

6. How you treat your own mistakes.

You worked late last night on a report, and you hand it in the next day without proofreading it. Only later do you realize that you misspelled the same word throughout the entire report. You pride yourself on being a perfectionist and are mortified that the mistake is out there for everyone to see. With each person who comes to you to discuss the report, you feel the need to point out the mistake and explain how it happened.

7. How you react to the hurt feelings of others.

You see a co-worker giving customers the wrong information about whom to go to with their problems. It's not exactly your business, but it bothers you, so you inform her of her mistake, plus several others she made yesterday. You introduce your remarks by telling her you are only trying to be helpful. Instead of thanking you, however, she is insulted that you interfered and that you seem to be looking over her shoulder. You feel rebuffed and are determined never to help out again, even if she asks you.

8. How you handle office politics.

Two managers at your firm hate each other. They never miss an opportunity to make the other one look bad. Whenever one of them catches you at the water cooler, he engages you in conversation and steers it toward his adversary, hoping to wheedle something from you that he can use against the other. You can see what he is doing, but whenever you give him ammunition, he becomes very friendly and indicates how much he enjoys talking to you. You like the intimate gossip, and little things slip out that you know are none of his business.

9. How you handle a crisis.

Your organization announces that at the end of the week, there will be a ten percent cut in staff. While you know you are not one of the people being laid off, you have to deal with the fear and anger of those who are. As one person after another comes in to talk it over with you, all your other work starts piling up on your desk. The crisis is making your head spin, and, before long, it begins to take its toll. By Friday, you are quick-tempered and have no time for anyone else's problems but your own.

10. How you participate as a team player.

At a round table meeting, everyone is talking about the new campaign. You have a lot of good ideas yourself, but every time you try to speak up, you suddenly worry that others will steal your ideas and run with them, leaving you high and dry. You know you have to contribute something to at least appear to be an active participant, but you keep the best to yourself.

11. How you react to favoritism and envy.

Every morning your boss passes your desk with a cursory hello. To John, who sits in the next cubicle, however, he steps in, sits down, and talks baseball scores for ten minutes. Every time a great new project comes up, the boss picks John to head it and places you second in command. Even John knows you are just as capable as he is, but he is not about to turn down a good thing when he sees it, so he continues his early morning sports chats. You don't know how to fight back, but you are brimming with resentment over both John and the boss, and you share your anger with almost anyone who will listen.

12. How you respond to change.

For years now, you have started work at eight-thirty in the morning. At a planning meeting, the managers realize that they need some people to work a slightly different shift in order to meet the growing work load. They now want you to begin at noon and work until eight at night. While this means making a few adjustments at home, it really isn't too much trouble and you can certainly use the raise in pay. However, you drag your feet about when you will start this new routine because you really don't want to do it. You're used to the routine you've got now, and it will be uncomfortable to adjust to a new one.

Step Two: Evaluate

Recognizing Patterns and Their Consequences, and the Core Beliefs That Fuel Them

Take a good, honest look at what you have observed about your own internal and external reactions to the things that come up at work. Is your way of handling problems helping you or hurting you? Let's go through the above twelve examples one by one and see what we can learn from them. What might be some of the underlying beliefs you hold that keep you caught in the same maze of behavior?

1. How you deal with conflict.

Pattern: When someone does something that continually annoys you and strikes you as unfair, instead of expressing your feelings directly to the person who can do something about it, you spill them all out on others. You once again avoid conflict through off-hand remarks designed to let your anger out without ever having to go through an awkward confrontation with the one you're having the trouble with.

Result: There is constant, unstated tension between you and your co-worker because the source of the conflict never gets addressed directly.

Core belief: "Others won't take me seriously, so why should I bother."

2. How you handle criticism.

Pattern: Whenever somebody criticizes you, you feel that they are making you wrong. To discourage them from doing it again in the future, you put them off by being cranky or sarcastic.

Result: You make it difficult for people to offer you constructive criticism and information that you really need. It hampers your job performance and ability to get ahead because it is perceived that you are not easy to work with and don't want to learn.

Core belief: "If someone corrects me, he thinks I'm stupid. That is a personal attack, and I have to defend myself."

3. How you take in compliments.

Pattern: Whenever people offer you praise, it actually pleases you, and you are proud of yourself. But you immediately become worried that you will be perceived as conceited and stuck-up. To counter that, you try to display modesty by letting the air out of the compliments as if you don't believe yourself worthy.

Result: People are less likely to let you know when you are doing a good job since you don't seem receptive to their comments. Most people are far more likely to be critical than complimentary anyway, so you are depriving yourself of the little bit of positive and supportive feedback available to you.

Core belief: "Always act humble or people will think you believe you're better than they are and they will try to cut you down to size."

4. How you respond to the demands of others.

Pattern: Because you are uncomfortable with saying no and feel you need to always give people what they ask for, you end up trying to do everything for everybody.

Result: You end up not doing quite enough for anybody because there is not enough time, and you don't get your own work done.

Core belief: "The only way I can get people to like me is if I say yes all the time and give them what they want."

5. How you deal with an unruly boss.

Pattern: Whenever someone in authority puts you on the spot in public, you feel so ashamed that you get a frog stuck in your throat and can't say anything to defend yourself.

Result: You look like a person who takes abuse from others without standing up to it. Your co-workers respect you a little less.

Core belief: "People in authority have all the power, and I have none. There's nothing I can do when they act badly."

6. How you treat your own mistakes.

Pattern: You cannot tolerate people noticing your errors because it seems to invalidate you as a whole person.

Result: You are far too hard on yourself, and punish yourself for small and insignificant things. In assuming that others see your mistakes as harshly as you do, you defend yourself unnecessarily.

Core belief: "People who make mistakes have a character flaw and are inadequate."

7. How you react to the hurt feelings of others.

Pattern: When you see someone else doing the job wrong, you have a genuine need to be helpful and set them straight, but you tell them too many things at once so the other person feels bombarded. You speak about their mistakes in a way that lets you get it off your chest, but makes them feel bad.

Result: You end up creating an environment where when you have feedback that would actually be useful to others; they never want to hear it because of your delivery.

Core belief: "When someone rejects what I am telling him because his feelings get hurt, he is just being a baby. People should toughen up and take their criticism in whatever form I give it to them."

8. How you handle office politics.

Pattern: The charm of other co-workers seduces you, and even when you know it's not a good idea, you cannot help currying favor. You dismiss the long-term consequences of your harmful gossip and settle for the short-term booby prize of flattery and attention.

Result: In any office dispute, you are perceived as someone who changes sides easily and is disloyal. Nobody trusts you.

Core belief:. "People will only be attracted to me if I fill their needs."

9. How you handle a crisis.

Pattern: When things get tense and those around you are going through strong emotions, you get caught up in the drama and don't take time for yourself. You try to be all things to all people.

Result: You lose the perspective you would gain from stepping back, assessing the situation, and evaluating what you could actually do to make things better. You get over-extended and let down not only yourself, but all those you were trying to help.

Core belief: "When things go wrong, I'm responsible. If I don't take care of it, nobody will, and then everything will really fall apart."

10. How you participate as a team player.

Pattern: You think of your ideas as a hoard of gold that you have to hold on to at all costs. Even though you are working with a team, you are acting only for yourself.

Result: People can tell when others are holding back. In return, they do not feel generous with you. They are unlikely to share their wealth with you, and they are not inclined to pick you as someone they want to team up with.

Core belief: "If I put my ideas out there, people will steal them and get all the credit, and no one will know how smart I am."

11. How you react to favoritism and envy.

Pattern: Life is a horse race. When the horse in the lane next to you pulls out in front, you assume it is going to win, so you give up without a fight. The only prize you get is the consolation prize where you get to neigh and whinny to the other horses back in the corral about how unfair it all is.

Result: You look to others like a whiner instead of a fighter. They don't get a chance to see how capable you are underneath, because any time your competitor seems to have the advantage, you drop out of the race without showing your strengths.

Core belief: "He has it better than I do, so why should I try? I don't have a chance anyway."

12. How you respond to change.

Pattern: Once you have settled into a pattern of life, you sink into inertia and hate the idea of change just because it *is* change.

Result: By refusing to recognize the inevitability of change and make it work for you, your own inertia makes everything harder than it actually has to be. In the end, you are always lagging behind your own life.

Core belief: "Comfort is the most important thing. If that gets disrupted it is a terrible thing, so change should be avoided at all costs."

Step Three: Change Your Mind-Set

Working on Your Core Beliefs so You Can Move Forward and Get What You Want out of Life

Many people resist examining their core beliefs and doing something about them because they find the process threatening. It feels as if these long-held ideas are the bedrock of reality, and if they are challenged, the world will fall apart.

I know that challenging them is not easy, but I encourage you to press forward anyway. Don't be surprised, though, if you can't do it alone. Below are some suggestions that will help you reach out to others so that you can take the important risks.

1. Assume that some of your own patterns will be invisible to you.

Don't be afraid to ask others to point out what they see so that you can gain a new perspective. Make it safe for yourself by saying ahead of time that you don't want to be verbally attacked, but that you do want the truth.

2. Write in a journal every day.

Millions of people do this because they find that it helps them be more aware of their thoughts and actions. By going back to old journals, you can see how long the same pattern has been rearing its ugly head. It may not be pleasant, but you will really learn something valuable.

3. Talk to your siblings and possibly other family members to share memories.

You may very well find that you have many of the same indelible beliefs. Through examining your family history, you can uncover answers that will help you all.

4. Find a support group.

There are many people out there who are trying to resolve the same issues you are. You can be a great support to each other.

5. Gather together one or two friends who also want to focus on changing the beliefs that sabotage their lives.

Have a coffee and dessert night and exchange suggestions for handling your problems more wisely.

6. Seek the guidance of a therapist.

Certain issues may be causing some serious damage to your life, and you are intimidated by the idea of even looking at them. Therapists are trained to help people look at the most difficult things fate throws their way and work through them. They know how to make risk taking a little less menacing than it seems.

7. Take seminars and read books on this subject.

They will inspire you, educate you, and give you the extra support you need.

We always seem to be able to come up with a good reason to put off self-examination. But when you stop to think about it, no reason is good enough. What could be more important than expanding your horizons and freeing yourself from the chains that hold you back? Look at it this way: if you do it now, you have the rest of your life to enjoy your freedom.

When tackling big issues at such a fundamental level, you have to be vigilant and strong, but at the same time patient and compassionate with yourself. This is a serious journey, an undertaking that will shake up your life. It is like going from the ease of the Barcalounger in front of the TV to an expedition through a forest in Peru. The expedition isn't comfortable. You will have to charge yourself up for it. But once you go, you will never be the same again. The sights, sounds, smells and aliveness of the real forest are a vastly different experience than looking at a forest on the Discovery Channel.

Expect resistance. You are in the habit of being the way you are, and habits are not broken without a struggle. Studies have shown that to change even a small behavior, it takes at least twenty-one days of continued practice and of implementing the new behavior. By staying focused and changing one core belief at a time, you can accomplish a lot in a year.

As new issues and feelings come up, especially if they are completely unexpected, you may feel like you want to run and hide and stop all inquiries. This is the time for patience and compassion. Guilt, shame, confusion, frustration and self-hatred may all be there. You may even begin to feel that you are being disloyal to your parents by questioning your upbringing and, consequently, their values. These things all need to be looked at because they can pose the greatest barriers to personal growth.

In the course of changing the beliefs you have now, try replacing them with new ones. It's as good a time as any. As you progressively recognize what *doesn't* work, you will become increasingly aware of what *does*. Write it down. Put it into practice. This wisdom is coming from *you*. You no longer have to cheat yourself out of a rich and full life.

Today, we are lucky. Once upon time long ago, people were stuck with their conditioning. The whole idea of actually studying the mind that studies everything else, of examining how it works, and then making wise and conscious changes, didn't arise until the twentieth century. Math, architecture, biology, medicine — all are scholastic traditions that have been around for thousands of years. For some reason, it didn't occur to us until recently to focus our attention on our own minds, on the science called psychology. And it's a good thing we finally did, because now we are no longer confined to values we learned, and notions we picked up, before the age of reason. Now we are not limited to our parent's beliefs, or our church's, or the culture's.

There are available to us a plethora of ways that point to a path of wisdom, awareness, and change — therapy, consciousness books, spiritual books, inspirational speakers, and support groups. All we need is a little courage and an open mind. If you take a look around and you are daunted by the choices, just remember that a hundred years ago you wouldn't have had any choices.

Autobiography in Five Short Chapters

One: I walk down the street.
There is a deep hole in the sidewalk.
I fall in.
I am lost . . . I am hopeless.
It isn't my fault.
It takes forever to find a way out.

Two: I walk down the same street.
There is a deep hole in the sidewalk.
I pretend I don't see it.
I fall in again
I can't believe I am in the same place.
But, it isn't my fault.
It still takes a long time to get out.

Three: I walk down the same street.
There is a deep hole in the sidewalk.
I see it is there.
I still fall in . . . it's a habit.
My eyes are open
I know where I am.
It is my fault.
I get out immediately.

Four: I walk down the same street.
There is a deep hole in the sidewalk.
I walk around it.

Five: I walk down another street.

Portia Nelson, ©1980

SUMMARIZED POINTS

1. Ineffective childhood messages — core beliefs — ruin many adult lives.

2. Changing harmful core beliefs is a worthwhile endeavor.

3. As adults, we remain attached to core beliefs we absorbed when were under the age of ten.

4. Adults need to create healthy principles they want to live by.

5. Guilt is a gift that keeps on giving, and the gift is not good.

6. Amusement fills a human need and balances the serious side of life.

7. When tackling big issues at such a fundamental level, you have to be vigilant and strong, but at the same time patient and compassionate.

8. Create a self-portrait of yourself as you are today through focused awareness.

9. Recognize patterns, their consequences, and the core beliefs that fuel them.

10. Change faulty core beliefs so you can move forward and get what you want out of life.

CHAPTER THREE

STRESS AND THE WORKPLACE –

MANAGING FALLOUT FROM FRAZZLED LIVES

*"Fatigue is often caused not by work but
by worry, frustration, and resentment.
We rarely get tired when we are doing
something interesting and exciting."*
— Dale Carnegie

Can you identify something that is as debilitating as heart disease, causes as much time out from work as the common cold, and is more widespread than cancer? If you answered stress, you are right. In a nationwide survey, the Mitchum Report on stress revealed that most Americans are under much more stress now than they were even five years ago. Of all visits to primary care physicians, from 75 to 90 percent are for stress-related complaints, as are more than half of the 550,000,000 work days lost annually because of absenteeism.

Research has proven that the leading source of stress for adults is their jobs. The World Health Organization calls job stress a "world-wide epidemic," and the United Nations refers to it as "The Twentieth Century Disease." If you are still not convinced, consider this: A 1994 report from Roper Starch Worldwide, Inc. named "The Dream in Danger" showed that job satisfaction among about two thousand workers surveyed was at its lowest in twenty-one years. In 1973, nearly four in ten workers deemed themselves "extremely satisfied" at work, while today it is only one in four.

Certainly, stress is not only an American problem. In fact, the entire industrialized world is affected. A United

Nations International Labor Organization report reveals that "waitresses in Sweden, teachers in Japan, postal workers in the United States, bus drivers in Europe, and assembly line workers everywhere, have all shown signs of job stress. No occupation or nation appears to be exempt."

Now that we've established the scope of the problem, we naturally want to know how to eliminate it. But first, let's take some time to define stress and discuss some of its ramifications. Dr. Hans Selye, a pioneer in stress-related disease, says that stress is "the nonspecific response on the body to any demand made upon it." In response to danger, excitement, a challenge, or any kind of change, adrenaline is secreted. The extra adrenaline secretion is not, in itself, harmful, but *can* be under the wrong circumstances. Consequently, Selye distinguishes between bad stress — distress — and good stress — eustress.

Eustress is healthy. It moves you forward both energetically and enthusiastically. In other words, you move toward what you *want* to do. I remember a job where I was responsible for all the public relations — publicity, media, events, articles and advertising. From the time I was hired, I had six months to develop and implement all of the plans for the grand opening of a new facility. What an exciting challenge! I was in charge of my own work, and I was able to use many of my favorite skills. Even though I put in long days — took my briefcase home at night, worked in my car en route getting my thoughts on a tape recorder — it never bothered me. I put on sixteen events in eight days for the new facility. Was I tired? Of course. Was I distressed? No! It was great fun.

Bad stress, on the other hand, makes you feel anxious, irritable, negative, and lethargic. Author Jeff Davidson describes it as "a reaction to some type of pressure, either external or self-imposed, which prompts psychological and physiological changes of an undesirable nature." It is either mentally, physically or emotionally disruptive and occurs in response to adverse external influences.

Although we might not like to believe this, the symptoms of distress can actually be acts of kindness. You may take exception to my saying this, but I do so because these symptoms are the physical warning signals our body uses to get our attention when we have pushed ourselves too far. They are the red lights on the train crosswalk that warn you that if you don't get out of the way, the train is going to run you over. If we can become aware of the signs, if they push us hard enough and force us out of the wrong work environment, then they have actually done their job.

If you have experienced physical symptoms that you cannot explain, you might begin to ask yourself questions on a more philosophical level. "Is this really a simple headache or am I working against my soul?" If you find yourself absent-minded and constantly tripping over things, have you really just gotten clumsy, or is your life moving too fast? Are the hives you keep breaking out in a reaction to something you ate, or a reaction to the man at the desk next to yours who complains so much he makes everything around him turn sour? When these signs are ignored and needed life changes are not made instead, people lose more than their health — they lose peace, happiness, and the ability to enjoy life.

Allie

> *I tried everything to get rid of my sleepless nights, stomach aches, and lower back pain. At one point, I was going to a hypnotherapist, a massage therapist, an acupuncturist, and a chiropractor all at the same time. My body was crying STOP to the punishment of pressure-filled days. True, my work ethic had made me the top salesperson in my entire company, but I never seemed to reach a plateau where I felt I could rest. In my business, there were always quotas. You could go from hero to zero in a month, so you had to constantly push to make the next sale.*

It took a series of illnesses to alert Allie that her career path was ruinous to her health. Since she changed jobs, she has thrown out her bicarbonate of soda, sleeps well, and no longer needs an army of healthcare professionals to keep her well.

Stressed for Success

There are other signals that people miss all the time, like getting in accidents. It may seem to be a random event — driving through the garage door — something that could have happened to anyone, but that may not be the most accurate explanation. At any given moment that we are extra vulnerable, we are making ourselves susceptible to an error in judgment that can be costly indeed. Don't wait until you end up on a hospital gurney, at a police station answering questions, or at home recuperating from injuries, to pay attention to the signal, understand it, and act on its meaning. A serious mishap could be telling you to slow down, to value the preciousness of life, or to pay attention to the here and now instead of always worrying about the next production meeting. If you ever find yourself at home recuperating from such an accident, use the time to contemplate whether what you are losing in time and money are really the most important things to you, and whether it is time to make some significant changes.

Another thing that can result from stress is addiction, which is a clear signal that something in life is off balance. It could be something in your personal life that is amiss, but for many, it is their professional life they should look to as the source. Unfortunately, addictions are confusing because on the one hand, they try to caution us to stop in our life track, and on the other hand, they numb us so we can pretend no alarm is going off. Whenever we exhibit an obsessive need to fulfill an out-of-control habit like alcohol, tobacco, drugs, and so on, it means we have shut down our warning systems and shut out our lives.

The Impact

Stress is a warning signal that tells us we are out of alignment physically, psychologically and emotionally. According to research, the problems below occur on a daily basis as a result of it.

All too often, we resist the obvious signs and keep going on the way we have been. What can result has a serious impact on either the heart or the brain.

"I was only forty, and my hair was turning gray. Since I've stopped running around in circles for my work, my hair has literally turned brown again."
— Peter

The Heart

"More heart attacks occur Mondays between six a.m. and noon than during any other time," says cardiologist Harry Dassah. "Psychological stress, like the kind that occurs during busy periods of your life or during a major change, does have an impact on the health of the heart."

Under stress, the heart beats faster, the body releases more fat into the blood stream, blood sugar concentration increases, and the body secretes chemicals that accelerate the blood clotting mechanism. All this puts you in line for a heart attack. And if you have a heart problem or a family history of it, you need to be extra careful.

A new study of heart patients demonstrates that high levels of mental stress in daily life more than double the risk of myocardial ischemia — an insufficient blood supply to heart tissue — that is often a precursor to heart attacks.

"My partner and I were in so much stress that we had to take aspirin every day for headaches. Then we got ulcers from the aspirin."

— John

"This is the first time the degree of risk associated with stress has been documented," says lead study author Elizabeth C.D. Gullette, a doctoral student at Duke University Medical Center's Behavioral Cardiology Laboratory in Durham, North Carolina, "and we were very surprised at the importance of negative emotions in triggering ischemia, as well as the size of the risk."

The feeling that many have of being an indentured servant on the job is now being looked to as a large source of strain on the heart muscle. The Institute of HeartMath (IHM), a non-profit research and education organization located in Boulder Creek, California has demonstrated scientifically that the heart talks to the brain in significant ways. The heart has its own intrinsic nervous system and its own functional "brain" which talks back to the main brain via the nervous system. A person who is content exhibits a smooth electrocardiogram, indicating cardiovascular efficiency and nervous system balance; a person who is frustrated produces a jagged graph. IHM has also demonstrated that even bunnies get irregular heart function when around people who are stressed.

The Brain

The impact of stress on the brain shows up as a rise and fall of the neurotransmitter *serotonin*. As many of us know, this kind of fluctuation can dramatically alter our quality of life. Recent studies with human and nonhuman primates suggest that fluctuations in the level of serotonin play an especially important role in regulating our level of self-esteem; high serotonin levels are associated with high self-esteem and low serotonin levels with low self-esteem. Our level of serotonin is also responsible for mood swings, brain functioning, and impulse control. Possible consequences of insufficient serotonin are irritability, over-reactivity, and lowered brain acuity, resulting in dropped productivity. Compounding the problem is the fact that the very environment that produced the stress in the first place will demand that we continue to be productive in spite of depleted resources.

A more serious biological toll that results from too much stress on the brain is the overproduction of cortisol, which causes brain cell death. When the brain cells die, the brain is starved of its only source of fuel, glucose. This in turn can lead to slow cognitive decline.

PHYSICAL	EMOTIONAL	PSYCHOLOGICAL
headaches	anxiety	poor concentration
tension	anger	boredom
insomnia	bad temper	confusion
stomachaches	crying spells	dullness
proneness to accidents	fist pounding	negative self-talk
hives	depression	forgetfulness
dizziness	mood swings	spinning mind
restlessness	bad dreams	lethargy
colds/illness	frustration	low perception of reality

Anxiety Producers You Can Work On

Your heart, your brain, and the rest of your body do not know or care that you are getting paid big bucks for this project, or that you need to win that contract, or that a prize position in a new and growing department is up for grabs next month and you have to beat out fifteen other candidates if you want to secure it. Your body just knows it needs to slow down. The impact on the heart and brain are only two of the major medical problems that stress can cause. Other stress-related disorders include cancer, cerebrovascular disease and colitis.

Of course, life is not a smoothly paved road. I am not saying that it is, even if you have the best job in the world. There are ruts and potholes all along the way for everyone. Many adversities cannot be avoided. They need to be experienced, accepted, and eventually overcome so that we can move on. But other adversities can, and should, be met as a challenge, as an opportunity to flex our muscles and become stronger human beings. The point here is that the workplace is one area in which we can exert control far more than most of us realize. If stress cannot be eliminated, it can at least be reduced.

The following are thirteen anxiety producers you *can* work on and do something about.

1. Your job doesn't use your inherent talents and skills.

You are a biological success. Your DNA has crafted your unique set of talents and skills enabling you to engage in wise work. Now, all your biology asks is that you use its gift. When our inherent traits are not used, or when they are dismissed, it causes stress because we are not actualizing our personal potential. In other words, we are stifling ourselves.

2. You lack the necessary skills to do your job.

There is nothing more anxiety producing than going into work at eight in the morning and having to bluff your way through the day because you really don't know what you're doing. The whole time you're trying to pull the wool over everyone's eyes, you are also having to figure out how to do the job right. You feel like an impostor, and you're always worried about being found out. It's a vicious cycle. The fact that you are making so many mistakes because you don't know what you're doing constantly undermines the self-confidence you do have and makes you believe something is intrinsically wrong with you. It doesn't take many weeks on a job under these conditions to get you to feel you are a generally stupid person.

"Half of my job involves typing, and I have no coordination in that area at all. After doing it for about an hour, my head just pounds, and I get very grouchy."

— Sally

There isn't anything wrong with you. The problem is that you never should have taken a job that is a mismatch with your own skills. Some obvious examples are a waitress who can't balance a plate, let alone a tray of food; a telephone repair man who has vertigo; an accountant who was never good at math; a grade school teacher who doesn't like children; a copy editor who isn't nitpicky.

3. Working against your values.

Your fundamental values and beliefs are etched into your brain. You can't change just because someone with different values is giving you a paycheck — but many try. At work, they are expected to perform against their convictions, and as a result, they go through a great deal of inner turmoil. Even in this age, when you can barely find the word *integrity*

45

in the dictionary, it is still a basic part of our human make-up. One way or another, going against our values chips away at our conscience, producing self-loathing, agitation, sleeplessness and ulcers. If you are trying to sell term insurance to a twenty-three-year-old who doesn't need it and can't afford it, just to fill a quota, it will probably come back to haunt you. Knowing that your employer, an HMO, is passing the buck to customers for services that were part of their cost-saving contracts will nag at you at the most unlikely of times. We can try to fool ourselves into thinking we didn't have any choice, but some inner voice will remind us that we ourselves did not take the high road.

4. Work relationships.

People can be both wonderful and frustrating, sometimes both within the same sixty seconds. It is natural to get along with people who have the same temperament and values as we do, who have a pleasing personality and good work ethic and make our jobs easier. However, when we take a job, we are not given the opportunity to peruse the employee list and select who should stay and who should leave based on our own personal preferences. To some degree, we take what we are given, and we are *given* them for eight to ten hours a day. Somehow, we have to make it work for us, and sometimes people forget that in compromising to make it work, they still have rights of their own. They're still entitled to stand their own ground. In other words, they don't have to remain quiet and put up with everything just to please those around them.

> *"No man is an island."*
> — *John Donne*

Most people tend to tip one way or the other. There are those who try to have everything their own way and those who are too timid or well-mannered to make *anything* go their way. Obviously, what is best is to strike the right balance.

Without good work relationships, we feel isolated and alienated. Some of the people who attend my workshops tell me of feeling like outcasts; others say they are constantly misunderstood; still others say they feel invisible because whenever preferences are being aired, they are always outvoted. It would be so much better for everyone if people would simply remember the golden rule during difficult times. The wisest way to evaluate any situation at work when there is a disagreement is to consider what is best for yourself, consider what is best for the other person, and then go for a win/win agreement.

5. Conflict.

In my seminars, these are some of the things I hear people say that constantly get on their nerves:

- The people around me are too loud. I'm trying to think.

- They're so bossy. They never leave me alone.

- She's too slow. Can't she move any faster? I'm on a deadline.

- He's such a know-it-all. I can't ask a simple question without getting a lecture.

- I hate the it's-not-my-job type of people who will never help out unless they have to.

- He is so negative. I can't stand hearing him complain one more minute.

- If that woman puts on any more perfume I'm going to gag.

- The guys want the radio on all day tuned into that awful easy-listening music. Don't they know what decade this is?

- He sits there and picks his teeth. He has the most annoying personal habits I've ever encountered.

- It makes me nervous the way those people gossip. I know they're talking about me whenever I'm not around.

Managers often report that the biggest time drain of their day involves resolving what seem like little conflicts between people. Here are some basic skills you can use to avoid or relieve conflict in your own environment:

a. Listen actively.

This conveys to others that you care enough to really hear what they're saying. An effective way to do this is to wait until they are finished talking, then rephrase what you heard them say. You do not have to agree with what was said. You are simply indicating that you got the message.

b. Give appropriate feedback.

It is usually best to approach the person privately. Ask her permission to give her feedback by introducing your remarks with, "I notice something that isn't working here. I'd like to help. Do you mind if I give you some suggestions about it?" Then gently, and nonjudgmentally, tell her your observations. If the person needs it, offer to support her in making a behavioral change.

c. Voice your complaint to the person who is personally involved.

Don't complain to everyone else in the workplace and make them part of the problem. That only causes more stress all around. When you do voice your complaint to the appropriate party, make sure you separate the person from the problem. Just because one thing is wrong does not mean you need to make the whole person wrong. After you have factually but gently stated your complaint, ask the person to explain his side, and then decide together how the problem can be solved.

d. Accept differences.

We often assume tacitly that we are so right about things that everyone should think exactly the way we do, even though we know we are all born with unique differences. If you can become more open and accepting of the differences between people, you will go a long way in creating equanimity and decreasing stress wherever you are.

e. Balance emotions with reason.

When we respond only with our emotions we tend to be coming from the most impulsive side of ourselves. As we know, we often live to regret our impulsive actions. They are narrow, self-involved and they only exacerbate conflicts. If you sense that a storm is brewing, and you want to pick up the heaviest object in the room and hit your co-worker with it, that is not the time to air your differences. Schedule a time and place in the near future. Ahead of time, practice the words you will be using so that you know you are going to communicate just what you mean to say and not spill out every single thing that has ever annoyed you about the person.

6. Trouble with bosses.

Research shows that one of the most stressful work conditions an employee has to contend with is a strained relationship with his boss. Employer/employee relationships are front-loaded with problems because they are never equal. Bosses can fire you; you cannot fire them. So you not only have to do your job well, but you have to get along with them. In many cases, that means you decide to let them be right in situations where you know they aren't. Or, you have to make a concerted effort to tell them they are wrong in a way that doesn't make them feel criticized. They're paid to know more than everybody else, and they feel they need to keep up the appearances that they do. Over time, this can put a strain on a relationship, even one that is basically sound.

Here is a list of typical complaints I hear from people in my workshops:

- Whenever my boss explains something to me, he uses a condescending voice as if I probably won't understand him if he speaks to me like an equal. Because I am a woman, he uses kitchen metaphors to make his point: "You know how when you're cutting vegetables you go from the left to the right? That's how I want you to divide up these items."

- I'm not saying I'm perfect, but if she has to point out a mistake to me, why does she have to do it in the middle of the reception area where everyone is listening?

- Management has totally unrealistic expectations about how long it takes to perform a task because they've never been on this end of the business and actually had to physically perform the task themselves.

- It's heartless the way my boss won't let people with children take care of family matters when it's really important.

- I understand that he is in a cranky mood because of the pressure his bosses have put him under, but that always means the rest of us have to walk on eggshells around him. It's not as if we aren't under the same pressure he is.

- There are a number of things I know more about than she does because I deal with them all day long. She makes snap decisions, and she is often wrong. It's really hard to tell that woman when she is wrong.

- It doesn't matter how well this department performs, management never shows their appreciation. They don't encourage us to be creative even when they can see from past results how much our personal creativity contributes. We also don't have access to any encouraging coaches or mentors, and that would be a great support to us.

All of these are legitimate complaints.

One reason we get into trouble with our bosses is that we believe it is up to them to establish the parameters of our work relationship. Instead, employees need to learn how to be proactive in developing that rapport. They need, as much as they can, to view their relationship with their boss as they would with another co-worker — two people trying to get a job done. If they can find a basis to truly like each other, all the better. When people like each other, they handle differences and misunderstandings in a more peaceful manner.

Remember, bosses are just human beings like you. They have their strengths and weaknesses, good moments and bad ones. They may also have pressures that you are not aware of, for they have bosses, too.

To avoid tension with your boss, build your reputation with her as a competent, cooperative, and productive employee whom she can count on. It is a common misperception to think that the boss is dripping with power and the employee is helpless. But the truth is that it's not so black and white. She is caught between pleasing the higher-ups and getting the people she supervises to perform. There may be times when she feels far more helpless than you do.

Here are some ways to amend a damaged relationship with your boss:

- *Provide solutions, not problems.*

  Bosses need all the help they can get. If you can show them how a problem can be solved, you will win their confidence and trust.

- *Be complimentary.*

  Bosses need acknowledgment, too. When you notice that they are at least trying to be fair and helpful, show your appreciation with a thank you.

- *Be your own public relations person.*

  Sometimes bosses are too busy to see the fruits of their employees' labors. In the course of a work day, it's possible to let them know in various ways. Report your accomplishments at a meeting. Write them up in a memo.

- *Clarify your boss's expectations about an assignment.*

  When you are given new work to do, be sure you understand your boss's objectives and goals so you are not working at cross purposes with each other.

- *Honor time constraints.*

  Remember, your boss is as busy as you are, so keep meetings short and to the point. You don't want your boss to be afraid to let you in his office because you'll keep him hostage all morning.

7. Fear of job loss.

There can be a number of reasons why an employee fears losing his job. Some things he can control, some he cannot. If your company has been downsizing or is simply going out of business, there is virtually nothing you can do to keep your own job. The crisis is bigger than you. However, if you had a conflict with your boss or have not been performing your job up to standards, you have the power to turn things around.

At those times when we cannot control whether we are to be let go, we *can* dictate how we will deal with our fears of such an occurrence. We have a choice. We can either let fear take over and paralyze us or take action to dissipate it. After all, the only things that are really frightening you are your own thoughts.

Instead of conjuring up all the "awful and terrifying things that could happen," keep your fear in perspective and try to understand its role. Fear has its purpose. It is present in both man and animal to help them flee from danger and to set appropriate limits so they will not get hurt. The idea is not to try to get rid of your fear, which is there to help you, but to use it wisely to avoid making serious mistakes.

One psychological tool you can use to help you work with your fear, so that it works for you and not against you, is to stand outside yourself a moment and observe yourself as part of the scene that's being acted out. Notice how your fear makes you more reactive and less capable of practicing critical thinking.

8. Powerlessness.

In their studies, Essi, a San Francisco research firm, demonstrated that the four biggest self-care skills that are the core of stress management programs — eating well, staying physically fit, not smoking, maintaining a desirable weight — actually have a negligible effect on people's ability to cope with work pressures and rapid change. The only factor with any significant impact on a person's ability to withstand work pressure is their personal power. More on this will be discussed on page 62. For now, let us just say that some of the most common indicators of a lack of personal power for employees are:

- The general work environment is one in which there is tight control.

- Employees have no autonomy over how they produce their product or provide a service.

- No one listens to their solutions or to their problems.

- They are not consulted when either work or roles are redesigned.

- They are not consulted about how much work they can actually take on.

- They are given breaks and lunch hour times that conflict with their own needs and the needs of the job.

- They are required to work with faulty equipment that keeps breaking down, and are still expected to stay on deadline.

- Employees are not "in the loop" enough to get all the information they need. They are not told the organization's goals so they feel isolated and help-less.

- They are not allowed to contribute their own ideas.

- There is either too much structure or not enough structure for a particular job.

- People do not have access to much-deserved promotions because they are not invited to hang around in the right circles at work.

Perry

I deliver washing machines and dryers for an appliance company. Sometimes, I have to pull that dolly up a flight of concrete stairs just to get to the foyer of a building, and the machine gets scratched on the cement. They're supposed to give me a second guy to help, but they usually don't. They're supposed to give me the better, more sturdy dollies so the machines don't get damaged, but they're too cheap to buy enough of them. And I still have to deliver each machine on time so I can move on to the next job. They expect me to be careful, even though I don't have time to, and they expect me to do the job perfectly, even though I don't have the equipment to do it. At the end of the day my nerves are wound up tight because there's no way for me to get out of the straight-jacket the bosses have put me in.

9. Conflict between work and home schedules.

Your daughter is in her first dance recital, but a production line has just shut down, and you have to get it operating again. You want to take your kids to the beach, but you have to work every weekend in the foreseeable future. You want to watch your baby take her first steps, but the family needs the extra income, so you need to get a job, and she has to go into daycare. Sound familiar? In America today, millions of families are making such heartbreaking decisions, and there never seems to be a right choice. Career women, especially, feel like a ping pong ball, bouncing back and forth between practical financial considerations and considerations of the heart. This creates untold anxiety and guilt.

Liz

I am a mother of three. I work ten-hour days five days a week and it takes me fifty minutes to drive to work — each way. As a lab technician, I have to complete a certain number of tests per day, and if I don't do them right, some poor patient won't know he has a deadly disease. I don't feel like a superwoman, but I have to act as if I am, to fulfill my many roles — employee, bread-winner, mother, wife, housekeeper, and planner of the family's social calendar. No matter how I try, my kids never get enough time with me. Something's got to give.

The most important thing Liz could do for herself right now is to sit down and take a good look at her own values. It is so easy to get stuck on a merry-go-round that doesn't seem to stop, and not realize that you can actually get off. If you want to shake up your thinking so you can get your life in focus and make strong, wise decisions, ask yourself this: "If I were on my death bed looking back over this period of my life, what would my regrets be?" When people are on their death bed, they never say, "I wish I'd spent more time at the office." What they regret is not having loved and cherished those around them more.

If you feel stuck spending too many hours away from your family, just stop and evaluate whether it's time to change jobs. Sometimes we have to take stock of ourselves and make sure our lives are aligned with our values.

10. When the job expects you to be all things to all people.

Have you looked in the mirror this morning? How many people did you see? If you saw one, you are doing well so far. Now, ask the image how many people it is trying to be at work. One of my clients was managing a staff of thirty, filling in for two people who were on vacation, and letting her boss cry on her shoulder about his marital difficulties. She doesn't have enough time to remember who she is, let alone what she needs to be doing at what time. This would be crazy-making for anyone.

If you're in a position where it's demanded of you to be ten people instead of one, you need to recognize that it's not in your DNA to be ten people. To be kind to yourself, you need to honor your own honest limits. People get caught up in the *I have to* mentality and forget they have the right to say no when what's being asked of them is too much. Recognize your right to stand up for yourself and declare what your needs are in a particular situation. Go into your boss's office; list for him all of your responsibilities and how long it takes to carry them out, so that he can actually see that there aren't enough hours in the day to do it all. Ask him to prioritize your projects in order of importance or deadlines. Or say, "These are the ten things I'm supposed to do today. I only have time to do seven of them. Which seven do you want?"

11. What you do is who you are.

While conflict between work and home tends to be a woman's issue, identifying with one's job tends to be mostly a man's issue.

From a very young age, boys are taught to identify with what they do, and girls associate themselves more with their emotions. In some ways, this may make males work hard and achieve more, but it also sets them up for great personal disappointment when the recognition they get at work does not match their self-image. If you feel that you are one of those people who measures himself solely by what he does for a living, take an inventory of your life, and see what kind of toll this attitude is taking. When work is all-consuming, we become one-dimensional, and then we are basically at the mercy of the workplace for how we feel about ourselves.

Joan

I had a boss once who worked very hard, but he wasn't very popular so he missed out on an important promotion he should, by rights, have gotten. When I walked into his office, I saw him sitting with his head buried in his hands. Without looking up he said, "Why am I completely devastated by this? When you missed a promotion, it bothered you, but you shook it off and went on with your life." I knew what the difference was. Part of my identity was that of secretary. But I was also a wife, a friend, a soccer coach for my kid's team, and finally — a person. My boss could only think of himself as an engineer.

Try to remember this: You are not your job. You are not what you do. You may contribute a wealth of expertise to your job, but there are other parts of you that are just as important. When we are in tune with who we truly are, we do not come unglued if things fall apart at work. Of course, we would prefer that everything roll along smoothly, but when we know who we are, we have a core of strength from which to withstand disappointment and hardships.

12. Hassles.

The daily accumulation of hassles is sometimes more stressful than any one major event in a person's life. Little things add up over a period of time and can drive you bonkers. As we all know, they start when you leave the house for work in the morning — no newspaper; then you don't pay attention to the speed limit and you get a ticket. From there it's all downhill: no parking space in the employee lot; somebody in the office forgot to brew the coffee this morning; there are ten messages on your answering machine — all from people *complaining;* someone else took the vacation slot you wanted to sign up for; your desk is covered with paper, and you can't find the post-it note with the phone number you're supposed to dial before nine o'clock. It goes on and on. You probably feel like a balloon ready to pop!

No one is immune from daily hassles; we are only subject to different dilemmas, quandaries, and predicaments. What can you do about them?

One: Recognize which ones you can't do anything about and practice serenity. There's really no multiple choice on this; that is pretty much all you can do.

Two: The problem is that too many people put things in the first category that don't belong there. They fail to discern that they *could* make a decision to make the situation better. They just don't want to face the decision.

Three: Look at the big picture. Have you ever seen a roller coaster that goes up but not down? That's how life is. If you can accept that taking a dip is inevitable, and that there will always be hills and valleys, the equanimity that comes with that attitude will stop the stress before it starts.

13. Burnout.

Burnout can occur even if you absolutely love your job. Anything that we are required to do every day on a schedule, whether we feel like it or not, sooner or later is going to burn us out. Our stress level can grow extremely high and many will not, or cannot, take the time to cool off.

When we use ourselves up in this way, we have focused too much on work and lost our perspective on life. The result is that our energy takes a nosedive, and to recoup it, we need to take a good long break or vacation. We need to put ourselves in an environment where responsibility is minimal. This is the time for self-indulgence and pampering — hang out in cafés, sleep in late, get a massage, and don't do anything you don't want to do. You don't even want the word *work* in your vocabulary.

Once you regain your sense of calm and your sense of self, you can return to your job, hopefully with the wisdom to avoid getting yourself in this mess again. People often use their vacations to get chores done around the house, but it would contribute so much more to their lives if they would use vacation time to rejuvenate themselves.

What Does the Future Hold?

After discussing all these anxiety-producers in the workplace, the question looms up: What can we expect down the road in the culture at large? Are the sources of stress going to go away? Every indication is that stress will continue to increase rather than decrease. Things are more complicated now than they were even five years ago, and people are under increasingly more pressure.

Computers were supposed to simplify our lives and save us time, yet the work week is longer now than it was in the fifties and sixties. Computers were supposed to mean a paperless society, yet never before have we printed out more paper since the *age of information* began. More of the printed word means only one thing — more for our poor overworked minds to take in. E-mail and faxes only add to the problem. Both give advertisers another line of access for junk mail, which we have to take the time to sift through in order to get to the information we really need.

Ironically, another source of stress in the computer era is the fact that it is so easy to *lose* information. Twenty-five years ago, when everything we needed to know was kept in a filing cabinet, the only way to lose it all in an instant was if there was a fire. Now it can disappear because there was a power outage while you were on-line.

One widely publicized source of stress at the end of the twentieth century, especially for those with not particularly technological minds, is the rapidity with which companies change computer programs and systems. Anyone who has ever worked in an office knows the strain it puts you through when you have just gotten used to one system and the company announces it is about to institute another, more cutting-edge system that will "help you do your job so much better."

And finally, the worst thing the computer age has done to increase stress is that it has changed our subconscious perception of how long it should take to get things done. If you are at a keyboard, information can be brought up in a nano-second. A human being cannot rack his memory for data that fast, and yet "computer time" has built up the expectation that there will be instantaneous results from every source, including the human mind. In addition, computers remember basic facts, whereas we tend to retain whatever emotional tone that went with those facts. This has been known to complicate decision-making.

Our minds and bodies have been functioning a certain way for millions of years. They are not going to operate on computer time just because we have invented computers. In the book *Data Smog*, author David Shenk quotes Nelson Thall, director of research at the University of Toronto's Marshall McLuhan Center as saying, "We're pushing ourselves to speeds beyond which it appears we were designed to live. Man wakes up today and electric technology speeds up his mind to an extraordinary degree, but his body stays in place. This gap causes a lot of stress."

Shenk also notes that a billion-dollar market for acid reducers has grown as a result of all the stress, strain, headaches and digestive problems. He sites tension, in fact, as one of our biggest growth industries. Two out of three visits to the family doctor are thought to be stress-related, and the three top-selling prescription drugs are for ulcers, depression, and hypertension.

How to Manage Stress

We cannot get rid of stress altogether, but there are many ways to manage it. One way is to control what you can and make peace with the rest. The second is to face your fears, especially the catastrophic ones. And the third is to pay attention to the stress reduction tips listed below.

Stress Reduction

1. Personal power.

A stress research firm found that of the twenty-one stress-related factors they examined in high-pressure work situations, the only factor that could predict who got sick and who stayed healthy was a person's perception of his or her personal power or lack of it. Personal power defines how much control one has over one's life, the ability one has to function and to express him- or herself. In your place of work:

- Do you have the freedom to suggest your ideas and have them be heard?

- Can you exercise autonomy over your own area of expertise?

- Have you been given clarity as to what is expected of you?

- Have you been painted a broad picture of how you fit into your organization?

- Are you allowed to say no when something unreasonable is being asked of you?

- Can you set boundaries around how much overtime you put in?

- Is support available when you need it?

If the place you work at does not provide these options, you may be surprised to find out that you can effect some real changes yourself. To increase your ability to get your message across to the powers-that-be in an effective way, be open, polite, and honest. When you talk to your boss, make a point of listening carefully to his response so that you are having a real two-way conversation. People, even bosses, want to feel they are participating in a conversation, not having a list of demands thrown in their face.

Your personal perception of work is within your own realm of power. Two people working on the same project can be under equal amounts of pressure, but react very differently based on perception. One can be busy, but upbeat and happy because she sees the project's importance and agrees with its design. Another person can be doing the same job, but be miserable because he is at odds with any plan he didn't choose himself, and in addition thinks the work is beneath him. Imagine how unpleasant his work day will be compared to hers.

If your own perception of yourself is cutting you off at the knees and causing you unnecessary difficulties, you might want to consider re-molding your attitude. You are not helpless to the ways of your own mind.

2. Communication.

Good communication is essential for preventing and easing tensions between people. These days, many corporations are structured around people working in teams toward a common goal. A man who ran his own small company said to me last year, "We don't *regulate* any more, we get people to *cooperate*. We don't govern, we persuade. We don't try to impose one way of seeing things on everyone, we build consensus."

To operate in this way, you need people skills. Whether you head a team or are a team of one, how effective you are at communication depends a great deal on how well you understand verbal and nonverbal messages from others. This means that when you are listening to other people talk, you read what else they're *saying* with their hand gestures, tone of voice, body posture, and so on. One of the main keys for encouraging cooperation and avoiding conflict in a group of people is simply the ability to understand what is going on, both individually and as a group, and then to act wisely. So any extra tools you can use to figure out what people are saying, both consciously and unconsciously, can only help.

Of course, to read other people you first have to read yourself, to know what *you* are feeling. Good communication begins at home. Now many people can easily tell you what they're *thinking*, but they are vague (if not downright wrong) about what they're *feeling*. I have seen people seething with anger who insist they're absolutely fine. If we're not in touch with our own emotions, we become easily reactive because they are in charge of us and not the other way around. We tend to misperceive what others are saying and can unwittingly cause unnecessary conflict. People who are aware of their own feelings have a much greater capacity to navigate their way through social gatherings at work, whether it is by the water cooler where a great deal of networking takes place or at formal meetings. They can take in information and make surer decisions on the spot.

In addition, people who are in touch with their own feelings and those of others exhibit empathy and sensitivity, both essential ingredients for communication. They are able to gain the trust of others. Do not underestimate the value of trust in the workplace. Bosses and co-workers not only turn to others who have the technical knowledge they want, they turn to those they trust. And networking, *the* word for the nineties and beyond, is based on trust.

The art of communication, then, has as its core the art of personal emotional management, which includes the ability to simply know what you are feeling at a given time. One who can manage his own emotions is not at war within himself. Consequently, he is less likely to be at war with others in his place of work. Peace of mind and good communication, then, go hand in hand.

3. Interpersonal work relationships.

Trust, respect, understanding, and compassion are necessary in any relationship. At work, where people have to function together as a team and reach a common goal, these values are even more important. They are the oil that makes the machine operate. And yet, co-workers often focus all their attention on their tasks and very little on how they treat each other. Taking the time and effort to develop good work relationships not only relieves stress, but can be a great support in buffering us from other stressful aspects of a job. An extraordinary amount of tension could be reduced in the workplace if people spent just five minutes out of each hour carefully considering how to get along with each other.

We need to teach ourselves how to treat people, and frequently we need to teach them how to treat us. We all know the golden rule. We learned it as children. But most people do not realize that the reasoning behind it is so central to human behavior that some version of it has been expressed in almost every religion in the world: Judaism, Buddhism, Confucianism, Hinduism, and Taoism, to name a few. The idea behind the golden rule is that it is not that difficult to figure out how to treat others — just look to yourself and what you would want. We are all so much the same.

4. Problem solving.

There are three things you can count on in life: death, taxes, and problems. And the whole premise of a job is that in one way or another you are getting paid to solve somebody's problems. Charles Franklin Kettering, scientist, inventor, and businessman, used to say that finding solutions only involved a change in perception, since the solution always exists within the problem. The task, he used to say, was not to master the problem, but to make it give birth to its solution.

Different problems require different skills. Fortunately, in today's world, a myriad of books have been written on this subject so you don't have to reinvent the wheel. Knowing the right problem-solving skills is like having a hammer to pound in a nail and clippers to cut a piece of wire; it means having the right tool for the job intellectually so that you don't have to stress yourself out trying to pound a nail in with a pair of wire clippers. At the back of this book I have listed a few books on problem-solving techniques. Check them out.

5. Flexibility.

Today's fast-paced world of work demands that we be flexible. This is true for executive management as well as receptionists. Priorities, organizations, plans, processes, and people are being continuously rearranged. You have barely enough time to get used to last month's change before this month's is on your desk. If you aren't able to flow with the changes, you will exhaust yourself fighting them. To stay sane and relaxed, you must be able to float along in the currents of the river, maneuvering *with* the current, not trying to go against it by swimming upstream. If a rock looms, you must steer clear and then regain your balance and keep your head above water.

How does a person flow at work? First, recognize and accept that things change. If you are a person who needs to hold on tightly to the status quo, you need to work on loosening up. Second, don't take it personally. Think of your organization as a space ship. It is constantly having to correct its course in order to "go where no man has gone before" in the marketplace, and you have to change with it. Third, be proactive. If something is fated to happen, then it will. You are in a better position to maneuver if you are primed and ready. Fourth, if you fiercely disagree with the changes being made, find out intelligently and in an appropriate manner what you can do about them. You are as much a part of your organization as anyone, and if you genuinely believe something is happening that shouldn't be, speak up. It may be of benefit to others beside yourself. Fifth, have a back-up plan which may, in some cases, mean leaving your company. People who know they are willing to walk away are in considerably less stress than those who believe they are trapped.

6. Anger management.

Another outcome of stress can be a tendency to heap unbridled anger and verbal abuse on others. Even when we are lost in the middle of a tirade, we know we are doing something extremely unwise. It is most likely to occur when we are on overload and have a hair trigger; one thing too many goes wrong, and we are off! Whenever someone is out of control, he is painting the least desirable picture of himself in front of others. It may feel good at the time to let off all that steam, but the repercussions are far-reaching, and he may end up having to soothe his co-workers' nerves for a long time to come.

Whenever we feel a surge of anger coming up, we need to back off and use concrete techniques to calm ourselves down. Otherwise, before we realize it, our anger is out of control, and we say and do things that are embarrassing, inappropriate or downright rude.

One way is to have a pre-thought-out plan of action with a few verbal reminders that you can say to yourself as soon as you feel the anger blossoming.

Step One: Get away from the scene of your anger as quickly as possible. Have a few sentences that you can say to another person like: "Excuse me, I would like to complete this conversation in a little while. This is not a good time. I'll meet you back here in ten minutes." Then take off. Go to the men's or ladies' room or walk around the block and regain control of your emotions. Or, if you can be open about how you feel, you could say, "I am beginning to feel angry. I need to take a time-out and come back to our discussion in a little while. Let's meet back here in twenty minutes."

Step Two: Now, gain your composure by a) counting to ten slowly. When you become involved in a left brain activity like counting, your right brain — the site of your emotions — takes a break; b) slowing down and relaxing your body and thoughts; c) taking some deep breaths.

Step Three: Examine the real issues behind the problem that caused your anger. Then decide how you would like to respond to the other person. Practice using factual statements about the issues instead of using loaded or explosive language. If you feel overwhelmed by anger as you rehearse the statements, take some more deep breaths and start again.

Step Four: Prepare your frame of mind and your attitude for a mutually beneficial outcome so that you and the other person find a peaceful resolution to the problem.

Step Five: Use humor by thinking or reading something funny. Laughter counteracts anger by releasing endorphins that revive your sense of humor and your humanness.

Step Six: Meet with the other person with your impulses in check, and your rational brain in operation. Calmly state your message factually. Listen to the other person's response and you will find resolution.

If you know you are one of those people who gets into truly uncontrollable rages, this method won't be enough. You need to learn stronger anger management techniques. If you don't, you may find yourself down the road facing a lawsuit.

7. Unrealistic expectations.

You can cause yourself heaps of stress by setting yourself up for disappointment with unrealistic expectations. You were planning on a raise when the company has frozen all its assets. You were set on getting a promotion when there are five people ahead of you who are more qualified. You expected total job security when you know your company is laying off hundreds of workers. Don't put yourself on this emotional roller coaster ride. Instead, try to be optimistic and realistic at the same time. In other words, understand that things may happen that aren't aligned with your own personal preferences. But you are resilient and will survive, and soon good things will happen again. That's how it works.

Of course this doesn't mean you shouldn't want or expect things. Just make sure you're not always longing for the impossible. There are times, however, when you can think big, plan, and go for the gold. The key is to know yourself, be wise to the ways of the world, and recognize which is which.

8. Bad attitudes.

Your attitude — how you make people feel about you and how you make them feel about themselves — can make or break your future. People with bad attitudes are not invited to participate in making decisions or working on new projects. They do not receive equal perks or get asked to interact with employees in a meaningful way. Their income and chances for advancement are directly affected by their attitude.

How is yours? Do you complain the moment something doesn't suit you, or do you take things in stride? Do you see everything in black and white so that you are always arguing with co-workers, or can you see a spectrum of grays? Do you get in people's way, or are you helpful and cooperative? Check out your own attitude by trying to see yourself through other people's eyes. Are you making them happy or miserable? If you need to, make an attitude adjustment. If you already have a great attitude, congratulations!

Here are some suggestions to help you improve your attitude:

- Be aware of your state of mind or the feelings that motivate you to negate yourself and others.

- Understand your influence on people's reactions to you.

- Cultivate the desire to change your disposition into one that contributes to the environment.

- Set small attitude goals for yourself, like smiling more or saying good morning to everyone when you walk into your workplace.

- Bask in the rewards that come from demonstrating a good attitude, like more acceptance from others.

- Make having a good attitude a self-perpetuating activity.

9. Lack of completion.

Not being able to finish a task can be extremely unsettling to a person who likes to shut doors and end sentences with a period. Most of us need some kind of closure around projects at work, even the little ones. It gives us a sense of peace, and if we don't get it, we are in a continual state of frustration. Completion is a key ingredient to satisfaction. Lack of completion is a key stress producer.

If you find yourself on a treadmill where you are always beginning new tasks before finishing old ones, try making a list of everything that is left hanging. Sometimes, writing it down and looking at it can make it seem more manageable. Then look at how you can structure your time to accommodate tying up those loose ends.

Here are some suggestions:

- Break down projects into tasks and tasks into subtasks.

- Make a list of both.

- Write out what actions need to be taken to finish off the tasks.

- Check off each task as it is completed.

- Count the number of tasks completed, and pat yourself on the back.

Sometimes, our pleasing natures or strong egos push us to promise others that we will accomplish grand things all within the allotted time. In the end, this is self-defeating because you are setting yourself up for frustration. If you continually promise more than you can deliver, you will always have a sense of being incomplete, and you will create the impression that you are unreliable.

10. Time to revive.

We are not built like machines. We cannot run with our engine revved up continuously. Eventually we will wear out. That's why we have coffee and lunch breaks — to keep from wearing out. It has been long-recognized that people need to take a little time off every few hours to revive their energy. Then they can return to their task with renewed enthusiasm.

If you are not getting morning, lunch, and afternoon breaks, you should insist on them. You have a right to them by law, and you need them so that you can take a breath and reconnect to yourself. And when you are on break in the café sipping your coffee, remember to take your mind away from your desk now that your body is away.

In many professions, taking work home is expected. But if you can help it, don't. Every now and then a project may take some extra time, but work should not be devouring your life.

What You Can Do to Reduce Stress on a Personal Level

The following are some little things you can do to ease some of the stress out of your life.

- Exercise three to five times per week for at least thirty minutes.

- Practice breathing exercises daily. Deep, soulful breathing is a good tool to use for calming down.

- Meditate to regain your own center.

- Get an ample amount of sleep every night.

- Listen to your body's signals and obey them.

- Cut down on caffeine and alcohol.

- Cut out smoking.

- Eat nutritiously, minimizing fat grams and calories.

- Play. Laugh. Entertain. Have fun.

- Take vacations, weekend outings, day trips.

- Include a higher power, spiritual connection, or positive philosophy in your life.

- Be grateful for what you have, and show active appreciation to others.

- Learn forgiveness — it will release a great burden.

SUMMARIZED POINTS

1. Stress is as debilitating as heart disease, causes as much time out from work as the common cold, and is more widespread than cancer.

2. Stress is a reaction to some type of pressure, either from an external source or self-imposed, which prompts psychological and physiological changes of an undesirable nature.

3. The symptoms of distress can actually be acts of kindness if we pay attention to their hidden message. A serious mishap could be telling you to slow down, to value the preciousness of life, or to pay attention to the here and now.

4. Addictions, which are clear signals that something in life is off-balance, are often a result of stress.

5. Research shows that one of the most stressful work conditions an employee has to contend with is a strained relationship with his boss.

6. A person's sense of personal power has a significant impact on her ability to withstand work pressure.

7. More and more people today are thinking about their life priorities and values.

8. Stress is a growth industry.

9. You are not your job.

10. To reduce friction in the workplace, first understand yourself and your own feelings, and then try to understand and take into consideration those around you.

CHAPTER FOUR

FINDING TIME TO FIND WISE WORK

*"Dost thou love Life? Then do not squander
Time: for that's the stuff Life is made of!"*
— *Benjamin Franklin*

"**W**hy am I not happy?" "Why is life a struggle?" "Why doesn't work, work?" We probe our soul with questions like these, but we will never hear the answers if we don't take time off in our hectic days to listen. Unless we slow down and take a deep breath, we cannot hear the subtle responses that come from within.

As we get older, the questions get louder. Teenagers and young adults may catch a whisper of such meta-questions, but they are easily diverted by temporary pleasures like the biggest blockbuster of the summer, or the latest video game, or the candy-red Pontiac Trans Am that just went on sale. As we get older, however, we begin to see our lives as a long journey, not just the step right in front of us. Questions about the nature and quality of life are bound to come up. By then, though, we are so mired in the car payments and the mortgage and the daily routine, and we are so used to looking for answers outside ourselves, that we fail to recognize the simple truth: We need to find enough quiet space so that we can listen to the answers locked deep inside. We need to stop and let them surface.

"Like tight shoes, you don't realize how your feet feel until you take your shoes off."
— Suki

Once we take that time, we can reflect on all we have done and all we hope to do, and decide if we are living the life we want or if, instead, it was programmed for us by others. Only then can we listen to our own voice, our own intuition, our own inner wisdom. Afterwards, when we go back to our busy life, we find that we are whole beings again, not walking machines. If we have chosen to take a break from our careers, the work we choose when we return will be right and satisfying.

In allowing ourselves *time off*, we can do all the things associated with childhood: play, dream, create, laugh, and grow. This does not mean we are throwing time away. Children are specialists at experiencing life, at researching, exploring other areas, being open to new ideas, and having a sense of adventure. All of these qualities that are still in us can be used as support for making a major change in our lives. The joy and sense of adventure directly counteract the fear that will try to stop us.

Roberta

My husband, John, was hard-working, dedicated, loyal, and upright — the perfect employee, but not such a perfect husband and father, I'm afraid. He was so wrapped up in his job that he forgot he had a life. During his career as a manager for a tool and die manufacturing company, he had two bypass surgeries. He would work ten hours a day, and even after that, he would bring his briefcase home so he could work at night. Whenever I suggested we go to a movie or take a weekend in the country, he would say, "I can't, I have too much to do." To that, he would always add, "We'll have time for that when I retire." Finally, at age sixty-eight, he did retire. Two months later, he died.

John thought he had all the time in the world. He didn't. Nobody does. Regardless of how we use it, time goes by and then it's gone. The combined power of every ruler in the world could not change that by decree. So in the end, the only thing that counts is *how* we used the time. Is what we're doing meaningful enough that if we were still doing it ten or fifteen years from now, we would be satisfied with it?

"My father's death made me realize I was mortal. It was the catalyst for my seeking work I love because it really hit me with the fact that you only have so much time. He didn't love what he did, he just did it because it was easy and he could make a living at it. At his funeral, I just knew I didn't want to make the same mistake he did."

— Harold

If you just keep going the way you are, ask yourself what you will miss and how it will affect you and the ones you love. If you are losing some of your spirit every year, what kind of husband, wife, father, mother, or friend will you end up as after half a lifetime goes by? If you need to take time off from work to stop the downward momentum, isn't it worth it?

The Right Place at the Right Time

Another advantage to taking time off from work is that it gives us some freedom of mobility. Usually, at noon on Tuesday we know exactly where we will be — in the employee cafeteria ordering a tuna fish sandwich and lemon meringue pie. But if we take time off and let ourselves explore, on a Tuesday afternoon we might find ourselves at a creative seminar on starting our own business. Or fly fishing. Or at a conference with teachers deciding how to improve our children's school.

When I moved to Sonora, I did not know that by taking time for myself, I was actually extending my personal and career growth. I was not aware of my needs or my reasons for escape. All I knew was that I had this inner voice, this intuition, which directed me to leave an environment that did not feed my soul, nurture my craft, acknowledge my contribution, or guide my growth. It was telling me to take the time to evolve to my next level. I had learned over the years that if I didn't listen to my intuition, I suffered the consequences. Needless to say, I had done enough suffering.

> *"It is never too late to be
> what you might have been."*
> — George Eliot

When we take time, we make space in our lives for those golden opportunities to find us. My time in Sonora, for example, cut down on the confusion of outside forces. I now had the peace, quiet, and time to let myself evolve. I was exposed to new people and activities that led me to my next career. I became the chairperson of the Tuolumne County Task Force on Self-Esteem. One day, I was invited to attend a program given by a motivational speaker. To my surprise, the man on the podium was talking about self-esteem — my own subject of interest — and he was getting paid for it! It had never occurred to me that speaking was an actual profession. I asked him how he got to do what he did. He told me to read everything, attend everything, and listen to everything on the topic of my choice, and then develop my own program. And I did. And I had fun. At first, I gave the talks to groups for free just to make some trial runs. I loved it and my new career was born. Not in a million years had I ever considered becoming a professional speaker. But I am one now.

Could that have happened to me had I not taken time off and gone to Sonora? I will never know. But I seriously don't think the change could have taken place under any better circumstances. When you have time off, a certain kind of natural evolution can take place, whereas, if you are perpetually chained to a full-time job, your time and efforts are prescribed by the job. While personal growth can take place in that setting also, an unstructured environment provides the freedom to view everything in a fresh way and to seize new opportunities.

I remember in the early seventies when companies were laying off engineers. At first, they were shocked, angry, chagrined, and fearful over a future they *had* believed was secure and planned out. Up till then, no one got rid of engineers! Yet after a period of time, they knew they had no choice except to look for other means to support themselves — nobody was hiring. As they began to explore their options, they found themselves channeling their misfortune into something constructive. I would hear about the engineer who had always wanted to be a carpenter and now was building cabinets. Or the one who had always wanted to be a chef who went to culinary school and was happily creating gourmet meals for one of the best restaurants in town. They might never have pursued these aspects of themselves had they not been pushed out of comfortable jobs and had the time to search in a new direction.

In the 1990s, thousands of people like those engineers lost jobs. Yet the majority have found a better future as a result. Many of their stories are in this book. I hope they will encourage you to recreate your life from the rubble.

Do You Have to Give Up Your Job to Find Wise Work?

Do you have to bail out completely, jump without a net, to find your next job? The answer is no and yes. No, if you can remain at work and still come up with the time to make your next move. Yes, if you cannot.

Joanne

I know this is the wrong place for me, but I don't have time to find a new job. I'm working sixty hours a week, commuting ten, and need to take care of the basics of life. I do send out a resume from time to time, but no one has called me.

Of course no one has called. Sending out a resume from time to time is no way to find a new job. Joanne has herself trapped into running in place. She has no time to focus on how to find a new job or even figure out how to make the job she has work better for her, because her every waking moment is filled with *I have to* and *What's next?* and *If I don't....* She is like a person with a low level of pneumonia who is always falling down the stairway. She is so busy getting her broken leg in and out of a cast that she doesn't have time to tend to her overall health and heal from the pneumonia. To find wise work, one needs to do more than aimlessly send out resumes. One needs a plan. To have a plan, one needs a sense of direction. To find the right sense of direction, one needs the time to find one's heart's desire. It is as simple as that. It all comes back to time. If Joanne had taken first things first and found out what she genuinely wanted, she would have a deep certainty of what she was going after. Consequently, she would conduct the proper research, make the right decisions, and take actions according to her goals. She would not find herself, year after year, working sixty hours a week with no end in sight.

To avoid making the same mistake, take the time to indulge yourself in self-discovery, learning, and application.

How Much Time Do You Have?

Believe it or not, we do have control over our destiny in many ways. But you need to be creative in finding ways to extract time from your schedule in the service of creating a new life. The best way is to chart the amount of time you spend at work along with your other activities. By writing it down on paper in black and white, you can see more clearly where to *steal* your own time back. Answer the questions below based on one month in your life.

Questionnaire

Fill in the blanks below.

1. I work ___ hours a week (include commute time).

2. I spend ___ hours a week with family and friends.

3. I spend ___ hours a week on entertainment.

4. I spend ___ hours a week reading.

5. I spend ___ hours a week volunteering.

6. I use ___ hours a week to sleep.

7. I use ___ hours a week to eat.

8. I use ___ hours a week to take care of other personal needs.

_____ Total

Take the total from this questionnaire and subtract it from 168 — the total number of hours in a week. Whatever is left is your time to invest in your future. If the number you come up with is less than five, start looking for a way out.

The biggest question most people ask is how they can take any time at all off from work when their family needs the income. Yet, there are ways to do this. You may have to bite the bullet and make do with a little less money, but think of it as making an investment in yourself.

Joe

I have been putting the same peg in the same hole at work for years now. I come home with a good paycheck, but I'm bored. I finally decided that I didn't need four TVs and my own Alfa Romeo. What I genuinely needed was a break so I could focus on my real needs. I decided to cut down the number of hours I keep my store open and contribute them to my life.

How to Get Time for Yourself

Here are some strategies for getting time away from your job while you explore your life options.

1. Ask Human Resources for a sabbatical.

Check the Human Resources Department of your organization and see if they have a provision for employees who want to take a set amount of time off work. Just because you haven't heard about it doesn't mean it doesn't exist.

According to a survey by the Society for Human Resource Management of 829 managers, about five percent of U.S. companies offer paid sabbaticals. Many more companies offer unpaid sabbaticals, but with the assurance that you can return to a job and a salary. These wise companies know that workers come back refreshed and more productive.

If you present this idea to management, and you are met with raised eyebrows, you might make the point that time off is not a new concept. The very first thing that happens in the Book of Genesis is that God works for six days, finishes his project (the entire universe), and then takes a little rest. The Old Testament uses the example of letting fields lie fallow every seventh year to allow the land to restore itself. Afterwards, it produces an even greater harvest. Most world religions have built in the practice of resting one day a week. There is a reason for this. Since ancient times it has been recognized that human beings need time for their souls and their inner lives. Weekends are supposed to be the modern answer for that, but in this day and age, they're not enough. Our lives are so go, go, go that we need a longer period of time to stop pacing the treadmill and reset our priorities.

> *"I didn't realize how tired I was until I stopped working."*
> — Nancy

Manny

For two years, I had been working on a major computer design project for my company. Once it was completed, my energy and attitude fizzled. I went into the Human Resources Department and requested time off before I started the next project.

Although my company doesn't pay when an employee is on leave, they do give him the time off and hold his job for him. I found that with accumulated vacation and sick days, and the willingness to not be salaried for two weeks, I could take a three-month sabbatical.

It was superb. When I came back, people asked me what I did for three months, and I happily replied, "Nothing." I told them I just hung out with my family, took a few weekends to go camping, read, tinkered with my toys in the garage and snoozed in my hammock. They looked at me as if I were crazy. But I'll tell you something, I did have time to think. And I realized that I like my company, but I'm tired of my job. So I'm going to be meeting with Human Resources again, but this time it's to reconfigure my career within the company.

If you want a sabbatical, find out if your company has made any provision for it. If they have, ask for one. Discuss with your boss how long you will need, and work out how she can cover your responsibilities while you are gone. If you go to her with a well-thought-out plan that answers her major concerns, you might be able to swing it.

Unstressing and Recharging

2. Get a reduced work week.

Find out if it is possible for you to work three or four days a week instead of five. Your income may go down, but by minimizing what you spend, your expenses will go down, too. If you decide you can handle a downsized lifestyle for just three to six months, you will increase the time you have to focus on your future by at least ten to twenty hours a week. Over a period of three months, you can accomplish a lot.

3. Telecommute.

If you work five days a week and spend two or more hours getting to and from work, you can buy yourself ten more hours a week just by working at home. That's about five hundred hours a year. With faxes, e-mail, Internet, and lowered long distance phone rates, it is easier than ever to maneuver this. And often, it works for your company also. They don't have to deal with as much people traffic in the office.

How to Use Free Time

Once we are presented with the gift of time, most of us are inexperienced at using it. Free time is a precious commodity, and we must not sit back and watch it drizzle through our fingers. The most important thing to keep in mind during this period is that you are in a state of renewal. With that as your central theme, you will have no trouble keeping your eye on the prize. The following are key aspects of this process.

1. Focus on your personal growth.

The term *personal growth* has been so overused, it is easy to forget how valuable it is. And you don't have to join a commune in Northern California or lie on a psychoanalyst's couch three times a week to do it. More than ever, there are resources available to help us look inward and contact our authentic selves. You can begin by asking yourself some pertinent questions.

- What is missing in my life that seems like a deep wide hole?

- Can I look at myself in the mirror and know that I operate with integrity? If not, what steps can I take to learn to speak my truth?

- Am I carrying emotional baggage from the past that ties up my energy and keeps me repeating the same old patterns?

- Are there childhood issues I need to resolve to be able to move on, both spiritually and practically?

- Would a little bit of professional help, in my case, go a long way? Is there a therapist I could see or a group I could join with like-minded people in it?

Janice

I had listened to my logical/rational brain for so many years that I felt like I was losing my femininity. I needed to reclaim it and become whole again. Instead of rushing right into another job, I asked for three months off. It was so obvious that this was what I had needed that I ended up taking eighteen months instead of three. During that period, I volunteered for several organizations. I made myself useful to the community, and it helped structure my time. In addition, I took nature walks and read about fifty personal growth and spiritual books the first year.

Every one of them sent the same message: I could not go on blaming my father for the time I spent in a business-like, rational mode of thinking. I had made the choice to be that way myself, and I was the one who would have to undo it. I did a lot of work around the relationship with the man in my life. In the course of doing that, I also built a relationship with myself again. Because I wasn't sacrificing all my time to a job, I had the time to focus on all the things that had long been getting in the way of my happiness.

In the past, I used to deny and repress my fears and problems or distract myself by staying busy. That is probably why they kept breaking through the surface of my consciousness and haunting me. But with my focus on personal growth, I am learning and using new tools to support myself.

2. Discover yourself.

You might say, "I already know who I am. I don't need to discover myself." Actually, self-discovery is not something you acquire once and for all. It is a lifelong process, and there is always more to learn. So to find the work you are meant to do, and take yourself to a new level:

Discover:

- Your buried talents and skills.
- The type of activity that naturally gives you joy.
- The kind of lifestyle that really suits your temperament.
- The misconceptions and limitations that stop you.
- The hidden passion you can apply to work.

Learn how to:

- Heighten self-esteem and personal mastery to find the tools you need to help you achieve success.
- Build technical, creative, clinical, and other skills needed to perform the work you plan to do.

- Increase interpersonal skills, which are extremely important for good working relationships with bosses and coworkers.

- Broaden your knowledge of the career and job marketplace as well as other avenues for finding wise work.

3. Increase your self-image.

When we have time to explore who we are as individuals, we learn important truths about our self-image. We find that all too often we measure ourselves by how others see us; we don't have an internal yardstick to measure ourselves by. For instance, after Florence was downsized from her corporate position, she began to question herself:

Florence

You ask yourself, what is your worth, what is your value? I used to have a title and a parking space with my name on it. Doors would open for me. Now, I am a horticulturist. Sometimes, when I go into a nursery and ask about plants, I get rebuffed. My first reaction is, "Don't you know who I am?" I have to keep my ego in check even though something inside me wants to say, "How dare you not answer my question immediately?"

When you don't wear the corporate uniform any more, you need to remember who you really are because you aren't treated with the same respect. Your reaction to people who reject you can tell you a lot about yourself. Sometimes, while I'm working in someone's garden, people will walk by and in my normally friendly manner I'll say, "Hi. It's a nice day!" I'm literally shocked that some people will turn away because of my grungy appearance. I may be grungy on the outside, but I'm not grungy on the inside.

When I'm all dressed up, people will say to me, "You don't look like a gardener." I ask them what I am supposed to look like because I am a gardener. I call on clients in my appropriate business attire, and I sometimes wonder how much of me belongs to me and how much belongs to other people's image of me.

4. Do something different.

Sometimes, we need to break out and do something dramatically different if we want to find out all the unfulfilled needs that never got satisfied.

Sally

I was the head of business development for a 550 million dollar company, and I was exhausted. So I asked for a year off from work to do something different for a while. I knew I would return with renewed energy.

While recuperating from a minor foot operation during my first few weeks at home, I saw a TV program on the need for foster parents. I decided that spending a year helping reunite foster children with their families would be a worthy use of my time. So I signed up for a ten-week program on foster care to learn how.

After completing the classes, they asked me if I would consider taking a baby in as a foster child. I blatantly said no. After all, I was divorced after nineteen years of marriage, and had never had any children. I had gone through all of the fertility work-ups, but had been unable to get pregnant. I thought I didn't know how to be a mother. And yet in some vague way, I still felt unfulfilled in this area of my life.

One day, I received a phone call from the foster care agency saying they had a two-month old child who was cranky and high-maintenance, and would I take him. I told them no, but offered to visit the baby, whom I found in a home with eight other foster children and two dogs. So I took him for an overnight visit. I swear, this kid looked me in the eye and said, "You take me and this is going to work out okay." I figured, what could I lose, because as a foster mom, you can say this isn't working and give the child back.

Well, the overnight visit has turned into eighteen months, and I love Jason so much that I'm in the process of adopting him. At fifty-years-old, I'm having another wonderful career as a mother. Unfortunately, I will need income to support myself and Jason, so I will be going back to work. But my priorities will be different now.

5. Take an extended trip.

Are there things you keep saying you'll do someday? Perhaps today is the day to satisfy those burning desires. Find the time to do something special for yourself. It will enhance your whole persona, attitude, and point of view.

Lane

I decided to take some time to travel before finding new employment. I mapped out a round-trip tour of the United States, bought traveler's checks with my small savings, got in my motor home, and took off with no time barriers. Because I had no deadlines or goals, I felt a tremendous sense of freedom from all of the issues that surrounded leaving my job. I had a beautiful adventure, regained my wits, and am now ready to start again.

6. Get guidance.

A personal guide — a career counselor, therapist, or career support group — benefits those who need someone to lead them through the maze of career and personal decisions. Let someone help you through the process of self-discovery, personal mastery, and reaching your goals.

Mavis

After I was laid off from my job, I bought fourteen professional books and was amazed at how behind the eight ball I had been. I had always just done my work and never taken the time to read about my field and what was going on in it. When you've just worked ten to twelve hours, the last thing you want to do when you get home at night is pick up a book on the same thing you've been staring at all day.

Counselors have an array of assessment and guidance tools to support people in pursuing new directions. There are also low-cost career centers in many areas that teach people how to put together a resume and attain interview skills. In this job market, there a number of important techniques to pick up if you want to get placed in a new and better position, and you probably don't know them all.

If your present career still attracts you, take workshops and read books on cutting-edge thinking and processes that allow you to increase your knowledge in your field. The more you know, the more attractive you are to an employer.

Some people decide to start their own businesses. There are many books, workshops and other resources, like the Small Business Administration, to also support them. Go to the library and bookstore and get on the Internet — all great resources for information.

To Make It All Happen, Use the PEP Method: Prioritize, Energize, Pace

1. PRIORITIZE what is most important.

Be vigilant about making yourself spend time on your priorities: the things you know add value to your life. Often, we perform the tasks that are in front of us, but forget the priorities that are out of sight. Before we know it, time has flown out the window.

2. Stay ENERGIZED.

Personal energy comes from enthusiasm and excitement about what you are doing. Keep a positive attitude, and your juices will flow.

3. PACE yourself.

Don't push too hard, or you will wear yourself out; yet don't move too slowly, or you'll lose your enthusiasm. Balance your goals with what your life allows.

More than ever, we struggle to find time to do all the things that will make our lives work. Yet years go by, and we don't achieve that which is most important. Time is now, life is now, work is now, everything is now, and it is now that you need to stop doing what doesn't work and go after the good life you deserve.

SUMMARIZED POINTS

1. Find enough quiet space to listen to the answers locked deep inside so you can assess and direct your life toward what you want it to be.

2. Regardless of how we use it, time goes by. The only thing that counts is *how* we use the time.

3. When we take time, we make space in our lives for opportunities to find us. And they do.

4. Most people who have lost jobs have found better ones to replace them.

5. Sometimes people who lose jobs find themselves.

6. When we are in the right place at the right time the right thing happens.

7. You do have control over your life and your destiny.

8. The term personal growth has been so overused, it is easy to forget how valuable it is.

9. You can't discover your lost self in the middle of a hectic life.

10. Prioritize what is most important, stay energized and pace yourself.

CHAPTER FIVE

WHEN QUITTING IS THE BEST OPTION

"And if you cannot work with love but only with distaste, it is better that you should leave your work and sit at the gate of the temple and take alms from those who work with joy. For if you bake bread with indifference, you bake a bitter bread that feeds but half man's hunger. And if you grudge the crushing of the grapes, your grudge distills a poison in the wine. And if you sing though as angels, and love not the singing, you muffle man's ears to the voices of the day and the voices of the night."
— *Kahlil Gibran*

What's wrong with this picture: Your bones creak as you get out of your car after the long stop-and-start drive home from work. After dragging your body into the house, you trip over a pile of laundry, spot the dishes in the sink and the chore list magnetized to the refrigerator, and think, "I'm too tired. Maybe tomorrow." You have just enough energy to find the TV remote and shove a popcorn bag in the microwave for dinner. When you try to fall asleep later that night your head is buzzing with all the things that went wrong during the day, what you still have to do tomorrow, and how you wish you never had to work again. Could it be that you are one of the thousands of people who hate their jobs?

You are the backbone of business. If it weren't for people like you, our whole economy would fall flat on its face. However, aside from a paycheck, you probably feel that the world does little else to recognize your worth. Most likely, your employer is not concerned that you find wise work, gain control over your job, or have a life. But you should be! If you find yourself spending more than one hour a day thinking, "Why am I putting up with all of this?" it may be time to quit.

"I was at the top of my organization and had all the privileges — nice cars, big expense accounts, in's with all the right people. But the politics, the schedule, and the demands sent me to the hospital emergency room more than once with chest pains. My wife finally said, 'I didn't marry you so you could die on me.' She strongly encouraged me to resign, and I did."
— Paul

Not every annoyance, of course, is a signal that it's time to leave where you are and move on. There can be many good reasons to stay. If the situation warrants, it is probably in your best interest to work things out where you are. This chapter offers both sides of the equation to think about.

Good Reasons to Stay Put

It is legitimate to stay if:

- You want to finish a project at work that you started because you feel responsible to the people who worked on it with you, and you need a sense of completion.

- You have not yet mastered the skills you need to take you to a better job, and want a little more time to learn them.

- Your present work schedule allows you to attend school, where you will get a degree that can take you in a new direction or to a better job.

- You've already worked there nineteen years and will be able to retire in eight months with a pension.

- There is one person driving you nuts, but you like your job, and you don't want to leave because of just one person.

- You are not ready to be active about making a change which will require you to learn to find a job, research your skills and talents, interview and negotiate salaries, and make new contacts.

- You need to expand your interpersonal skills, and your present work environment gives you ample opportunity.

- You are aware that you are taking the easy way out, and it would be better for you overall if you confront the problems where you are.

Should You Stay?

Below is another list of reasons which, at first, can sound just as legitimate as the ones above. Do some of these apply to you?

- You have heavy financial responsibilities.
  - ✧ a mortgage
  - ✧ your children's education
  - ✧ care for an aging parent

- You are a single parent with no other support.

- You are heavily in debt.

- You are very security-minded, and being without an income will cause you enormous anxiety.

These are not things to be dismissed; but, after careful consideration (and after reading this book), you might find that there are other ways to handle these issues, ways that don't take the same toll as a miserable job.

The next list is filled with excuses that you would be better off throwing in the trash bin:

- I have good benefits and will be vested soon.

- I'm used to this — at least I know what to expect each day.

- I might not like my co-workers, but at least I understand them.

- I'm afraid to take a risk.

- I don't want to go out there and face the unknown.

- My whole upbringing supported staying wherever I am and sticking things out.

- If I leave, I'll look like a failure and lose the esteem of others.

- I don't have enough of a financial cushion to fall back on.

- Right now, I have a short commute. If I leave this job, I may even have to relocate.

- I'm afraid of losing the high lifestyle I've gotten used to.

If you resonate with any of the items on *this* list, you may need to reexamine your thinking and find out what trade-offs you're making and how long you want to endure them. Do you believe there is no way out? Well, there is, and I encourage you to explore your options. There are far more than you think.

But first, to gain some perspective on whether it's worth exploring your options, write the answer to this question:

"If I do stay in my present job, what will my daily existence be like for the next five years?"

Now write the answer to this question:

"What are the benefits of taking charge and making a change right now? Is it possible that I can resolve my concerns and not let them block my way?"

Those were two fundamental questions designed to help you see the bigger picture. The following twenty questions are more specific, designed to point out specific trouble areas.

How Bad Is It? — Some Preliminary Questions

Circle the appropriate choice.

1. Do I like my job overall?
   always   *sometimes*   *never*

2. Am I comfortable with the people?
   always   *sometimes*   *never*

3. Is my workplace free of harmful stress?
   always   *sometimes*   *never*

4. Are there certain people I'm always trying to avoid?
   always   *sometimes*   *never*

5. Do I feel free to communicate when I am upset?
   always   *sometimes*   *never*

6. Am I treated fairly?
   always   *sometimes*   *never*

7. Do I feel I do a good job?
   always   *sometimes*   *never*

8. Do I feel in control of my job?
   always   *sometimes*   *never*

9. Am I satisfied with my role in the workplace?
   always   *sometimes*   *never*

10. Do I feel appreciated for my efforts?

   always   *sometimes*   *never*

11. Am I proud that I work for this particular employer?

   always   *sometimes*   *never*

12. Do I feel competent at what I do?

   always   *sometimes*   *never*

13. Is there potential for growth, both financially and personally?

   always   *sometimes*   *never*

14. Am I comfortable with my surroundings?

   always   *sometimes*   *never*

15. Am I treated with respect?

   always   *sometimes*   *never*

16. Does my job challenge me?

   always   *sometimes*   *never*

17. Am I free to contribute my ideas?

   always   *sometimes*   *never*

18. Am I afforded the opportunity to learn new things?

   always   *sometimes*   *never*

19. Do I get along with my boss?

   always   *sometimes*   *never*

20. Do I get to use my unique talents?

   always   *sometimes*   *never*

Now add up each category. If your aggregate of *always* is fifteen or more, consider yourself lucky. If your aggregate of *never* is more than five, think about whether you may want to start looking for another job.

Is Quitting the Right Answer?

By this point, you're probably saying to yourself, "This author really believes in quitting." Let me make the point that I do not believe quitting is always the answer. Sometimes I see people who desperately want to quit, but when I look at their work history, it is clear that they are always running away just when things start to get difficult. The difficulties are actually offering them the opportunity to grow personally, and they don't want to face that. Vexing experiences at work, when handled well, can be of great benefit to us because they show us areas where we have something to learn: communication, conflict resolution, better technical skills, and so on. If indeed the problems at work are a challenge to improve yourself, let yourself stay and get educated. Once you are at peace with where you are, if you still want to move on, you will be all the better for the education you've just given yourself.

Also, quitting is not meant as a way to increase couch potato time. Leaving a bad job is not supposed to be the golden opportunity to lounge around the house waiting passively for something better to come along. If the only time you're turning off the TV and getting out of the house is to play the lottery so you can win your "ticket to heaven," you are not using your time wisely. The best attitude to take toward quitting is that you are giving yourself the time and space to find out what you are meant to do with your life. Use that time to your advantage by taking action, not by vegging out. It is your future, and no one is going to knock on your door some afternoon during "As the World Turns" and present it to you on a silver platter.

No, quitting is not always the answer, but in my line of work, I see that it is the answer far more than people let themselves realize. I like to think of quitting not as a negative but as a positive. Leaving the *wrong* job is taking the *right* action. It is making the choice to advance one's own life. We are not just victims of circumstance. We choose our fate.

Some people might think of quitting as *just taking the easy way out.* Believe me, it is not an easy out. It takes great courage to leave a paycheck, benefits, and the other trappings that a workplace offers. It takes great courage to put yourself out in the job market again and go through interviews and possible rejections. It takes great courage to wonder how you are going to pay your rent and put food on the table. The old saying, "no pain no gain," does apply here. In its own way, staying and being a victim rather than taking a risk and venturing forth into new territory is taking the easy way out. Numbing yourself with booze and tranquilizers to cover up your misery is taking the easy way out. The people whose stories are told in this book have left work environments that disempowered them, and in doing so, increased their self-awareness and self-esteem. They now enjoy better lives. If they could do it, and if I could do it, so can you.

Reasons to Quit That Make Sense

1. You have the boss from hell.

In surveys, a bad boss is given as the single most common reason for job dissatisfaction. If you are not getting along with yours, and there is no way to resolve your issues, it's time to move on.

Some people just don't know how to handle leadership positions. They think being in charge gives them permission to be rude, pushy and inconsiderate. Have you ever gone into someone's office for a scheduled meeting and then sat there for ten minutes waiting for him or her to finish a phone conversation? Has a manager ever spoken to you as if you were a small rodent? Has your boss ever thrown a pile of work on your desk at three o'clock on a Friday afternoon, work she should have gotten to you by Wednesday, and asked you to have it ready by Monday morning? These are people who think they are the sun and that you are one of the planets revolving around it.

George

My boss, Alec, was a nightmare. I neither liked nor respected him. You never knew what to expect from the guy. One day, he would be pleasant, and the next day, he would squash you like a bug. Whenever I saw him, my body would tense up, so by the time I got home at night, my neck and shoulders were hunched up around my ears. Alec had me on a physical and emotional roller coaster. One morning, a good friend came to visit. After taking one look at me, he said, "Have you been ill? You look terrible." Until then, I hadn't realized how much putting up with Alec had taken its toll. In that moment I decided that enough was enough. It was like I had to be pushed against a wall before I could break free. I went in the next day with a letter of resignation.

2. The quality of your life is not being honored.

There may not be anything specifically wrong with your job, except the fact that it takes up twenty hours a day. It is simply eating up all your free time. We can get so caught up in the activities of the job, even when they are exciting, that we are beginning to *do* life instead of *have* a life. We are losing our humanness and becoming an automaton. If we're lucky, something comes along that shakes us up, something shocking and dramatic to knock us out of our reverie. In that defining moment, there is emotional pain, but that is what it takes to make us stop and reevaluate what we are doing with our lives.

Maria

I was a classic example of type A behavior. I worked ten hours a day while attending school at night to get my MBA, something I felt would add depth to my job skills. To meet all my obligations, I would have needed forty-hour days. My life was going by right in front of my eyes, and I wasn't there for it. Then, suddenly, three people in my life died, all around the same time. First, my sister, who was very dear to me, had an operation and didn't make it. That was hard. But I was so occupied with the busy-ness of my life that I didn't have time to really absorb that she was gone and that I'd never see her again. The next month, my secretary's mother died of cancer. Finally, a manager who reported to me was killed in an automobile accident.

By then, I was quite shaken. It somehow made me realize that I was not honoring the quality of my existence. I was giving more of myself to a job that didn't love me than to my husband, Joe, who did. And the organization I worked for had never recognized me nor compensated me for my level of contribution. Those three deaths revealed to me that when you die, no one is going to sit there and read your resume and care that you gave two hundred percent selling aluminum siding for thirty years. All of a sudden, it became clear that I was not having a life, and I left my job.

3. Your personal orientation doesn't fit in the organization.

Our personal style represents how we are oriented towards being in the world.

For instance, if you are:

- *An Extrovert*

  You are an expressive person, and you need to verbalize your thoughts and feelings. If you happen to work in an organization that is quiet and introspective, you may find the walls closing in on you by the end of the day. Extroverts genuinely need contact with people to juice up their energy. They need to interact with customers, work on teams, talk on the phone, and actively participate in meetings. Only by honoring this inborn social trait can extroverts actualize their creativity.

- *An Introvert*

  You have an active inner life, and contact with people often zaps your energy. You are more comfortable in a room by yourself doing your own job than at a meeting roundtable. In an organization that needs energy-filled, expressive people, you may not be appreciated or taken seriously because you don't broadcast enthusiasm. You get your energy internally, and to be creative and productive, you must be left alone.

- *A Logician*

  You like to thoroughly work things through in your mind, and you don't work well in a *do-it-now, think-it-through-later* environment. You need the time to analyze data and develop a plan. But by the time you're ready to distribute your fifty-page documents to the rest of the staff, they are already on to the next thing.

- *An Artisan*

  You are artistically driven and need to be creative, but you work in a job that requires number crunching. You can always see new ways of doing things, but your manager always wants you to do it the old way. When you go home at night, your right brain feels maligned and your left brain beats you up for having been inadequate. Again, there is nothing wrong with you. You are just working in the wrong place.

4. Your inborn talents and skills do not fit the job.

We are all born with natural skills and talents that dictate where we will be a success and where we won't. These are our strengths, and we want to be able to use them in our work. No one is strictly confined to her natural talents — one can always stretch to perform tasks one wasn't born to do — but this is like trying to use your left hand to perform tasks when you are a right-handed person. You can do it, but it's not comfortable. For instance, if you are:

- *A Visionary*

 Your job demands detail, but you are not a minutiae person. Your mind tends to take in the big picture, to see trends for the future, yet the management you work for can only see right in front of its nose.

- *The Analyst*

 Your job needs spontaneity and artistic flair, but your talent is to research and weigh data. Your focus helps decipher the specifics required to keep things on track, but to some people, you're not glamorous enough.

- **The Organizer**

You are an enemy of chaos. It is your natural inclination to keep things in order and keep them manageable. Your ability to structure the layers of a project supports the efficiency of your team's work.

- **The Mover and Shaker**

You can never sit in one place and be complacent. You are good at motivating people and at getting things done. If you work at a place that is under-ambitious, your talent for moving projects forward and starting new ones may be viewed as pushy.

5. You feel you are not treated equitably.

When we are dedicated and we give our best, it is insulting to discover that others are making more money, garnering more praise, and piling on more privileges. A resentment can build up that lessens our enthusiasm for our work and creates friction with other employees.

Sarah

I had been the vice-president of planning for an automobile manufacturer for over a year. One day, I found out that the man I replaced had made 25,000 dollars a year more than I was making. To add insult to injury, I learned I was actually the lowest paid manager in my organization. And here I was, managing all the revenue-producing departments! A month later, my workload doubled, but my salary stayed the same. Every time I sat down at my desk, I seethed with resentment.

6. People know you for the work you did before and cannot adjust to your new role.

People often get fixed impressions of who we are and what we are capable of doing. If they are used to you as an accountant, they will have trouble seeing you as anything other than that. You may know that you are a visionary and have real leadership capacity, but others will keep you pigeonholed in the same old position.

For instance, perhaps you worked on an assembly line, but all the while you went to college at night and finally got your degree. Now, you are ready for a promotion to a white collar job, but the powers-that-be still see the grease beneath your nails. Making a shift in thinking allows people to blossom in new directions, but not everyone is so open-minded, and their narrow focus can cause us to miss out on being offered fresh opportunities and getting new projects or promotions. If your present co-workers and boss still see you the way you *were,* then it might be time to start out fresh in another organization where you can recreate yourself in a new image.

7. Most of the time you're at work, you are bored with your job.

Even the best of jobs can get stale if enough time goes by. If you are in a position where there is no challenge or stimulation left, ask yourself if it is possible to stay where you are and make the kind of changes that will energize you and reactivate your interest. If you discover that nothing in your company will meet your criteria, it is time to go elsewhere.

8. There is no opportunity to advance your knowledge and skills.

The world of work is constantly changing. Remember typewriters and carbon paper? Our children will never use them, let alone know what they were. Remember when all written communication traveled by "snail mail"? Just try to do business with the Pacific Rim today without e-mail and the Internet.

A myriad of new ways to work are influenced by technological changes, up-to-date thinking, and new discoveries in the global marketplace. Look around and see what other people in your industry are learning so you keep up with your profession. If your job does not allow for professional growth, you may be pounding the pavement for a new job one day and come to the rude awakening that you are ten years behind the times. You must take on the responsibility for your own learning. No one will do it for you.

9. The work culture where you are employed has changed for the worse.

Josh

When the firm I worked for merged with a larger insurance company, little effort was made to blend the two corporate cultures together in a humane way. A minimal amount of information was shared about the changes to come, and there was no direct communication to prepare us for them. Everything that went on in that office suddenly got politicized, and it undermined the entire staff, including me. You could come in and find out a co-worker had been let go an hour earlier without any warning. It just wasn't a place I wanted to be anymore.

Let's say you just got a new manager, and his salesmanship style is more cutthroat; it puts pressure on all the other sales people to be the same way. Or possibly, your company has merged with a larger corporation and it's lost that family feeling. There are no special celebrations anymore, and they've made it difficult for employees to connect with each other. Or possibly, decision making used to be done at round-table meetings where everyone could throw ideas around, and now it is done through inner-office memos. In any of these cases, the result of the changes may mean that you just don't feel at home anymore. It's not the same company you originally hired on with.

10. The principles and values manifested at your workplace are not aligned with yours.

By laboring in an environment that doesn't practice what we preach, we can find ourselves laboring against our own soul. Sometimes, it is not completely obvious that this is a problem. To evaluate whether you and your employer are a good match in values, make a list of all your personal principles. Consider each principle. If you feel your employer's actions demonstrate that they support that value, circle it. This simple exercise should give you a clear picture of how your values match up. If the preponderance of values do not match up, you need to decide if you can live with theirs or if you need to leave.

11. You don't respect the way management is running things.

Can you count on your management to follow through on promises made to customers, or are you sometimes caught assuring people about things you know your company won't deliver. In other words, do they walk the walk and talk the talk?

Can you proudly talk to your friends and family about where you work? Workers need to have pride not only in the job they are doing individually, but in the company as a whole. If you don't have it, it will show up in your work and your relationships.

There are various ways in which management can confuse us and lose our trust and support:

- They don't deliver orders on time.

- Customer complaints are high because of poor service.

- They are laissez-faire about quality.

- You work hard to make your sales, but the product is never available on time, and you either lose the sale outright or you don't get your commission on time.

- Your company is not competitive in the marketplace and is seen as a loser — your career is suffering because of *their* lack of sophistication.

12. You feel physically ill, tired, or depressed when you are at work.

These things are all signs of stress and burnout. You must pay attention to them. When you are at odds with your work to a large degree, a myriad of physical symptoms will pop up to let you know in an indirect way what you might not be able to acknowledge to yourself directly.

13. You have made many efforts to change conditions for the better, yet nothing has worked.

You may have taken the initiative to meet with your boss and ask what you could do to improve your skills, meet her expectations, and elevate your status. Yet long after implementing her suggestions, you have still not been given better projects or a promotion. She does not invite you to important meetings, ask for suggestions from you in your area of expertise, or respond to your phone calls. You sense that she either doesn't like you or doesn't see you as valuable. After a while, this is bound to have a debilitating effect on your self-esteem. People want to "use" themselves at work, to have their qualities and skills put to good use by others, and when that doesn't happen, they stagnate.

14. Instead of *you* determining your career path, your company is doing it all for you.

Organizations will try to slot you where *they* need you. They don't necessarily consider whether the new position will help you reach new levels of expertise or whether it represents upward mobility. Today, with downsizing and constant change in most workplaces, you must take a far more active part in determining the direction of your career path than workers used to have to do. If the trajectory of your career is headed straight for nowhere at your present place of work, don't wait until they get rid of you. Take your future into your own hands.

15. You have inherited the "staff from hell," and they like it that way.

Leon

I was thrilled when I got my new job, so you can imagine how shocked I was when it turned my life upside down in all the wrong ways. On my first day, I walked into the belly of a people-eating dragon — a hostile sales staff who were angry with me for getting the job that each one there wanted for himself. The message was clear that I was not welcome. The rejection was very humbling and took quite a toll on my ego. I had always seen myself as a successful person, and then, suddenly I wasn't. At first, I thought I could get things to change, yet in hindsight, I can see there was nothing I could have done. They hated me long before they ever met me, and that was that.

When people are hired into supervisory positions, they usually inherit their predecessor's staff. This situation can be a setup for failure, especially if you as the new person have a different management style, are required to institute dramatic and unpopular changes, or if the job you acquired was one that someone else thought was rightfully his. If you walk into a hornet's nest, you are in for a hard time from day one.

16. You are in your own business and are tired of being responsible for doing it all.

As a sole owner, you are responsible for every single detail. You have to drum up new business, lick stamps, and keep track of receipts. You have to work eighty hours a week for the privilege of not having a boss over you. There may come a point when it's not worth it. Working for someone else would take the pressure off and actually be a relief.

17. You find yourself waiting for retirement.

Some people who are nearing retirement age have no spark for work anymore, and they're just counting the days until they can collect their pension. They are bored, unproductive, unenthusiastic, and just going through the motions until "R Day." They may still be extremely capable and rich in experience, but their energy has fallen, and it won't get up.

For some people, this state of lethargy represents a genuine reflection that they have put in enough years at work and are ready for time for themselves. The job is only draining the life out of them, and the best decision they could make would be to retire early instead of wasting more time. They may be able to either make more money doing something they've always wanted to do or might just want to go off and have some fun. If there is some concern about money, it's a good idea to check out your income options with your Human Resources Department before taking early retirement. Planning ahead of time is a wise move that will relieve anxiety.

Others who are soon to retire may want to seek out how they will be able to use their present skills to be of service to others after they no longer have to put in nine to five. After all, since our life span has greatly increased — men will now typically live to eighty-four and women ninety-two — we don't want to spend those last thirty to forty years parked in front of the TV watching "Dialing for Dollars."

Then there are those who don't really want to retire but are merely bored. They may find that they still have a contribution to make, like being a mentor to younger employees, sharing knowledge and history with other co-workers, or offering their wise perspective on all the changes that are taking place. By putting new life into an old job, those last few years don't have to be throw-aways. They can be an exciting time when you are entering a new phase of life, a phase where your experience really counts.

Should You Actually Leave?

The spaceship of tomorrow's employer may be waiting to transport you to a new frontier. But should you go? Should you stay? How will you decide?

Many decision-making processes are available. Which one you choose depends on your disposition and on how you operate. Some people listen to their intuition, an inner voice of guidance in their head that never lets them down. Others pay attention to their gut; they actually have a physical reaction when they are making the wrong decision. On the other hand, some people have a more measured way of coming to the right choice for themselves. They make lists, pro and con, and they evaluate the results. You've been around long enough to know which of these systems works for you. For those of you who prefer to be completely logical in weighing your objectives, I list some great decision-making books in the bibliography. Although intuitives have a sense of knowing, I've listed some other books to support their process as well.

If you come up with the resolution to **LEAVE:**

Let go of preconceived notions about how difficult it is to find another job and eliminate any other "hold-back" thinking. No one sets up obstacles in our path the way we ourselves do.

Elevate your self-esteem to a height where you are confident that you are doing the right thing and that you have the wherewithal to succeed.

Access your guts and fortitude and use them to move forward. Tap into that reserve you have been holding on to for a situation such as this and rev up.

Value yourself enough to find out what fulfills you, so you will find the fortitude to integrate wise work into your life.

Empower yourself to create a change that will move you to where you want to be.

Take Action

Now you are ready to take direct action. Make an appointment with yourself one day during the week for two hours. Use that time to put together a preliminary action plan — and I mean action. The key words are: what, when, and how. To move yourself forward, you need to be specific about what you are going to do, exactly when you are going to take which step, and how you are going to execute it.

Once you have made a decision, put everything you have behind it. You need to make sure you feel good about your decision so that you will continue to follow it through. Others, who often wish they could get up the nerve and make a decisive move, may try to second-guess you or fill you with doubts. This is something you need to defend yourself against so that it doesn't sap your strength and your resolution.

Author Wayne Dyer writes, "You'll see it when you believe it." Once you actually begin to make something happen, it becomes easier and easier to believe that the whole dream will come true. There is another saying: "Fake it until you make it." Act the part of someone who is competent and confident, and you will grow into the part. It is a "what if" game. "If I had complete faith in myself, what would I do next?" Go ahead and do that next and see how it makes you feel. And finally, keep giving yourself positive messages. A friend of mine gives himself smiley faces on a chart every time he prepares well for a job interview. Hey, we all need different reinforcement techniques!

When you know what you want to do, you will be amazed at how aware you become of a whole new set of possibilities. You will find yourself drawing the right people toward you and entering situations that will help you actualize your goals. But you need to be clear about what you want, or you will draw the wrong things.

Characteristics to Cultivate so You Can Leave

I know people who actually manifest the things they want in their lives. They are no different from you and me. What they do have are these characteristics:

- *Vision — great clarity about what they want*

They can describe their vision in detail and can realistically visualize themselves in their new conditions. The more they do this, the more possible, even probable, it seems that they will get there.

- *Strong intention — determination to get what they want*

They pursue their goals when they are thinking, writing, talking, exploring, reading, and being, as well as in their actions. They are resolute that they will achieve their objectives. They stay focused and don't let anything or anyone stand in their way.

- *Unwavering belief — a belief so strong that it stands up against challenges*

Other people, sometimes believing they are being helpful, try to persuade us to be *realistic,* meaning that we shouldn't aim too high. Successful people keep their goals high and their expectations in line. People may tell us we are being a *dreamer.* Successful people are practical dreamers. They have dreams, and they figure out how to make them come true.

- *Action approach — they know what they need to do and they do it*

If a person wants to drive a car, he gets behind the wheel. To dance, he moves his feet to the rhythm. To find a new job, career, or better skills, he researches his options, decides on a plan, and implements it. Everything requires movement. He moves towards his goals.

- *Focus — they stay on course*

They don't stop on the way or get sidetracked by fear or the myriad of other things that hold one back. Even the best get waylaid now and then, but those who are sure of the path they are on don't let themselves procrastinate for long. They just put themselves on fast forward and fly.

- *Faith — they truly believe they will get it*

They know it is just a matter of time. If things don't move as fast as they would like, if something goes wrong, if they get unavoidably sidetracked, it doesn't have a permanent effect. When they fall off the horse, they simply get right back on.

After you examine your work life and scrutinize it from all its various angles, you will see whether or not you should quit your job. If you determine that you need to stay, then use the opportunity to grow personally and professionally. If you decide to leave your job, then plan your escape with the advice in this book so that you have support systems in place. In either case, remember that you are on the road to becoming the wise worker you want to be and finding the best work life for yourself.

SUMMARIZED POINTS

1. Explore your options, and find ways to meet your responsibilities and have a good work life.

2. Don't use empty excuses to stay in job prison.

3. If you stay in your present job, ask yourself what your daily existence will be like for the next five years.

4. If problems at work are really a challenge to improve yourself, stay and get educated.

5. Leaving the wrong job is taking the right action.

6. Quitting is sometimes the only healthy, reasonable choice you can make.

7. People use different decision-making tools: intuition, a gut feeling or more measured means.

8. If you decide to leave, make an action plan that includes what, when, and how.

9. Feel good about your decision.

10. Cultivate the characteristics that help people manifest what they want: vision, strong intention, unwavering belief, action, focus, and faith.

CHAPTER SIX

WHAT TO DO BEFORE YOU LOSE OR LEAVE YOUR JOB

*"Your work is to discover your work,
and then, with all your heart,
to give yourself to it."*
—*Buddha*

In the 1930s in Hollywood, there was something called the "studio system." Many of you have heard about it. It signed up people like Judy Garland, Mickey Rooney, and Lana Turner when they were young and just ready to start work; it prepped them, trained them in their craft, took care of perks like insurance, and paid them once a month. When one movie finished, the studio lined up another one for them. They may have had to perform in a lot of Grade B movies that didn't match their talents, but they always knew there was work in front of them. Today, that's all over. Actors and actresses are on their own to seek out and find new projects to work on and negotiate their own terms. While that might mean they have more freedom to make their own decisions, no big parent in the sky is there to take care of them. And when one project ends, they have to scramble to get something else going.

The changes that took place in Hollywood mirror the changes in the global workplace in general. Good or bad, the age of job entitlement is over in the Western world. These days, you would have to look long and hard for someone who has been working for one employer for thirty years or more. (And then, it's probably a son or a nephew of the boss.)

121

The long-term security of an income, benefits, and perks over an entire career is gone. Instead, people must become self-reliant in advancing themselves in the workplace, and must realize that the only security they have is within themselves.

It is not within the cultural ethic today for employers to feel responsible for your future. Primarily, they have to stay focused on the bottom line — can they stay afloat in such a highly competitive world? The reason for all of the downsizing, mergers, and re-engineering antics of the past several years has been the need to continually refinance and cut costs. Companies all want to be as lean and mean as the next guy. According to the American Management Association, in a survey of one thousand companies conducted in June 1997, an estimated 60 percent said they would eliminate more jobs over the next year, adding to the more than three million layoffs already announced by U.S. companies during the 1990s.

Not that there aren't other jobs being created. The growth of new industries generates opportunities all the time, but you have to be ready to seize them. To take serious charge of your work life, prepare for tomorrow's opportunity today. Whether or not you can retire with a pension when you're seventy depends on how well you maximize your skills and work possibilities now. Nobody wants to outlive their money.

The surprising fact is this: With the rapid changes in technology, many employers expect employees to find new jobs every two to four years or they're considered dead wood. That's right, short term is in, and longevity is out. To be successful in the new workplace, you need to become a combination effective employee and job-hopper. The trick is to acquire a multitude of skills in a variety of work environments that make you more and more valuable each time you graduate to another position or company.

Moving Onward and Upward at the Same Company

Even if you feel fairly secure in your job, given the history of instability in the corporate world during the eighties and nineties, you are bound to have a few anxious thoughts as you're falling asleep at night. "My friend Jonathan thought he was set up for the next twenty years in the garment industry. Who would have known people would stop buying designer jeans?" Or, "What if they get a machine to take my place? That happened to my neighbor." Or, "My job could move to Taiwan." If you want more food for anxiety, all you have to do is read the *Wall Street Journal*.

The only thing for certain is that nothing is for certain. So just in case the worst is about to happen, to alleviate anxiety and a sense of waiting for the ax to fall when you are totally unprepared, read this chapter as if your future depended on it. Remember, you are always most effective when you're still relatively secure with your current employer. When you're on the calm part of the river, that's the best time to prepare yourself for white water rafting.

You will also find it empowering to take your future into your own hands. Waiting for someone in the chain of hierarchy to promote you, demote you, or remove you can make you feel like a cow standing in line at the slaughterhouse. If you feel helpless, unable to control your course in the whirlwind of market activity, you will make yourself far more susceptible to a "doom and gloom" mentality. Pessimism is not your friend. It will constrict your imagination and limit your possibilities. Think proactively and take charge of what happens next. If the best career move for you is clearly to seek upward mobility in the company you are at, here are some ideas to support you:

1. If you do not like your job, but you do like where you work, look for opportunities within the same organization.

If they don't exist, create them. You would be surprised at how many ways there are to do this.

Today's trend is to spend a shorter period of time in any one position, but to gain a wider array of experience within that job. To blaze a trail for yourself into a top spot, take the learning you gain from every position you are in and apply it in the next one.

"Being successful and making everything I do count is a big motivator for me," one woman said. "I was hired at my company as a communications director. I went on to manage the sales department, and I ended up heading the Human Resources Department. From the first job I brought conflict resolution skills with me, from the second I brought promotional skills. In the Human Resources Department, I use them both every day."

2. Find ways to keep your job interesting.

A colleague of mine, Gerard, had been with his company for sixteen years when he began to experience some frustration with his job, even though he mostly found it satisfying and rewarding. To stay where he was, but spice things up a little, this is what he did:

- *He helped reinvent his organization.*

   Gerard helped reinvent it four different times over the course of sixteen years. In fact, every time he did it and his job was then reconfigured, there came with it a new set of tasks to learn and skills to master. With each change he received a promotion. The scope of responsibilities expanded to keep his work day interesting, and his level of excitement high.

- *He got involved in a professional society.*

  This helped keep Gerard's skills better honed and his attention focused. He wrote articles for magazines and other publications which required a great deal of thought and caused him to conduct much-needed research. To his employers and peers, this proved he was talented and knowledgeable in all the areas he wrote about.

- *He got involved with his co-workers and helped them develop their own leadership qualities.*

  Spotting and developing talent in others is very energizing, and being someone else's coach can be equally rewarding. Gerard found that he had talent identifying people with high potential who didn't recognize it in themselves. He also found that in giving others a foot up, he added vitality to his own work. Together, these employees ended up making some very strategic contributions to their organization.

- *He made sure his life was one of continuous learning.*

  Staying in one place when everything around you is constantly moving is a risky business. Gerard developed an operating philosophy that enabled him to hit home runs with every curve ball they threw him. Each time his company tossed a change at him, he managed to turn it to his advantage by creating a new program with it. Meeting his challenges head on kept his work life from ever growing routine. If there had been no variables or reinvention, his life would have been boring. Many others have had the same experience.

Lois

In 1983, I was the first employee hired by WorkConnections, a temporary employment agency. Geoffrey Johnson, the president, had started the business in his home bedroom office, but soon realized he needed to go public, to venture into the marketplace so he could sell his services to a wider base. Someone had to look after the office, and as his secretary, I was assigned the task.

As WorkConnections grew, I hired a staff, and my opportunities for job growth increased. My job became quite diversified. I had to answer calls, contact customers, and set up new territories. The company kept growing. I then became the internal communicator, personnel director, educator, trainer, manager, and community contact. Needless to say, I was never, ever bored.

2. Offer to cross train in other departments so you can familiarize yourself with different kinds of jobs.

You will learn more about the organization as a whole, thereby increasing your skills and broadening your value across the board. Then, you may be the one that is too valuable to let go when layoffs occur. It is also a very effective way to get your name circulated.

3. Take a job within the company you don't particularly want and use it as a stepping stone.

Sometimes, it can lead you to what you *do* want. You may even need to accept a lower salary or job status. But remember, do this only as a short-term strategy, and be cautious about sticking around long after it is time to move on, just because you're comfortable. The purpose of the new job is to improve your abilities and make yourself known to those who can help propel you into the position you really want. It is not meant to keep you in a rut forever.

4. Volunteer outside your company for nonprofit organizations.

It may help you to hone new talents which you do not, at the moment, get paid for. Not only can you further develop yourself using the experience to help your career, but you will derive tremendous satisfaction from contributing to the good of others.

Mazie

I was a telephone operator when I decided to volunteer for the American Cancer Society. I got involved in helping on the logistics committee to plan and produce a major fund-raising event. Doing so taught me how major programs are orchestrated. Two years later, I put my experience to use chairing a major event for my company.

If I hadn't helped out at the ACS, I wouldn't have gained the confidence I needed to get involved in big projects and manage large numbers of people, nor would I have gotten the hands-on experience that has proved so valuable. All this led to my involvement in other company activities that I hadn't even considered. People have gotten to know me better now, and they see me in a different light. Last week, I was promoted to a job managing other operators.

5. Consciously build your relationship with your manager.

The relationship with one's boss can be one of the most important factors in determining whether a person moves forward or stays behind. In reality, there is no such thing as a company. That is just a concept. What there are, are people. People make decisions. The person at your current job most tied to your future is probably the one who directly supervises you. Even if this is not someone you would cultivate as a close friend, you can still cultivate a good and respectful working relationship. Make sure you understand what your contribution to the organization as a whole ought to be. Performance indicators should be understood in advance so expectations are kept realistic. Request ongoing, constructive feedback so that you know when you are doing well and when your performance needs improvement.

6. Build good work relationships with people from other departments.

You want to offer ideas, cooperation, and assistance where you can, yet you don't want to be an intrusive, pushy know-it-all. Try to be sensitive about what is needed and perceptive about what will be effective. Both of these people skills can greatly further your career. The irony here is that in this increasingly machine-oriented world, people who are socially adept have a distinct advantage over those who are technically adept because the ability to network is so important. Good networking involves building relationships *before you need them*. If a new position comes up, a desirable one, who do you think is going to be informed of the job — someone people have only spoken to in passing or someone who has worked with them in the past and demonstrated her value?

7. Find out about extracurricular training programs offered by your company.

Almost always, the Human Resources Department has pamphlets available indicating what kinds of classes are given during lunchtime, after work, or on weekends. They're always free, and something not enough people take advantage of. If your place of work has a newsletter, check there too. It is understandable that company memos informing us of classes and workshops go unread. So many things cross our desk each day, and often, all we want to do is get the in-pile to go down. But give interoffice paperwork like this at least a cursory glance to see what might benefit you.

8. Ask someone you admire to mentor you.

A person who has been around longer than you and knows the ins and outs of the business can be a great asset. It is important to remember, though, that in your eagerness to learn, you still need to be respectful of your mentor's time. Before you ask a question, make sure you check that it is a good time for the person to stop what he or she is doing and answer it.

Acquire the Habit of Lifelong Learning

> *"The illiterate of the future will not be the person who cannot read. It will be the person who does not know how to learn."*
> — *Alvin Toffler*

We all know how important it is to stay current on leading-edge information, trends, and technology in your field. If you have any doubts about this, open your Yellow Pages to find the plethora of trade schools, night schools, university extensions, and adult programs available.

You can also keep yourself informed by reading. There are business, trade, and personal-growth books, and whole sections at book stores and the library on almost any subject you may be interested in. In addition, the Internet adds a whole new and unimaginable dimension to the possibilities of information gathering. You can also attend personal and skill-building seminars, review professional and trade magazines, and listen to audio and video tapes on a variety of subjects to enhance your understanding and skills.

There are numerous professional associations that will place you with colleagues you can learn from, people who have similar interests and goals. There are associations for virtually every profession in America, from metallurgists to daycare workers, from computer programmers to sign painters. These groups are a great resource not only for information, but also for job referrals. Since they often have dinners and conferences, they are another source for networking in which you can develop important relationships. These get-togethers are a place to learn new techniques, find out about state-of-the-art materials and computer software, discuss customer problems, or pick up tips about how to sustain your small business.

Prepare Mentally for an Upcoming Transition

Everything we have talked about so far in this chapter has been directed at the person who is floating along in a very seaworthy vessel. She may know as a general principle that people get laid off, but up till now, at the place where she works, everything is just fine. Unfortunately, not everyone is in a boat that has no holes in the bottom.

Usually you can feel your feet getting wet long before the boat begins to sink. First, you hear the rumors around the coffee machine that new management is "trimming the fat." Then, there are hush-hush meetings you should, by rights be invited to, but aren't. Then, you find out about an important project coming up, and you haven't been asked to participate.

Any savvy person in today's work world knows how to tell when his ship is sinking. If you have some kind of undefinable feeling that it's going down, you're probably right. This unpleasant anticipation about being called into your boss's office and given the bad news is extremely anxiety-provoking. You could spend your time waiting for that moment by biting your fingernails and dipping into a snifter of brandy to steady your nerves. That won't help. What you need to do is begin to take productive action now while you still have a desk to work at and a paycheck to live on. It may be true that forces outside you can create havoc on your life. However, you are not completely at their disposal. Among other things, you can always work on your own mind and prepare it for the changes to come.

The mind is the most important tool we have during a major transition. By understanding your own psyche — what triggers it, what soothes it, what energizes it towards goal-oriented action — you can mentally prepare yourself for virtually any upheaval. Notice what sends you into a downward spiral emotionally and how you deal with it. When people get depressed, they have the unfortunate tendency to ruminate about how bad it is, and, worse, about how bad it's *going to be*. This kind of toxic thought process makes it virtually impossible to visualize new beginnings rising from the ashes. Life seems dismal and without possibility. Just when you should be up and running, preparing for life changes, you are paralyzed into inaction.

Some people are more susceptible to anxiety than they are to depression. A worrying mind cannot let go of the problem, and cannot help making it worse.

Katy

I could tell by what people weren't saying that the hatchet was about to fall. It would have been so much better if someone had told me what was going on, but no one did. I used to go home at night and do puzzles with my kids and all the time I was looking at the little pieces I would be thinking, "If I make any spelling errors on that proposal I have to type up tomorrow, it will affect my final job rating, and then when I do have to scramble through the job listings looking for another position, I'll have to take that crummy job rating with me. No matter where I go, it will follow me for the rest of my life. What if I can't get to sleep tonight? I'll be a nervous wreck at my computer tomorrow morning and completely mess up on the proposal."

A simple spelling error leads to ruination and homeless status within minutes. Most of what our minds come up with when we are in a compulsive state of worrying never happens. But people cannot take this fact in when they're still in the thick of it. If major changes are about to take place at work which will leave you without a job, pay attention to catastrophic thinking and take steps to eliminate it. Nice, quiet activities like reading sometimes don't work because they don't bring the nervous system down a couple of notches. One thing that has been proven to work time and again, however, is simple aerobic activity. It has a palpable effect on the nerves and brings you out of the chronic delusional state of worrying. Your rational thinking mind can kick back in and ground you in a state of reality. And in the real world, you can look for real solutions to your problems.

Keep a keen eye out for any kind of downward spiral. Try out mental, physical, and emotional strategies that disrupt depressed or anxiety-ridden thoughts and allow you to envision plausible alternatives to the catastrophic ends you have been envisioning.

Become Actively Involved in the Job Search Process

Here are five useful steps you can take to put yourself in the driver's seat:

1. Arm yourself with facts about today's job market.

The best time to look for a job is when you have a job. If for one reason or another you might be without one soon, begin the search process now. Most of us do not know how to go about a successful job search. Even more, we don't want to know. Let's admit it, it's no fun. We would avoid the whole thing if we could. All we want to do is send out a resume, go on one and only one interview, and get hired. *And live happily ever after...*

That simple approach does not work anymore. The job search process today is more sophisticated than it ever was before, and it takes a very active approach that requires time, energy and thought. Here are some reasons why:

- Most jobs — approximately 85 percent — are never advertised.

- Only about 15 percent of job seekers get jobs from the 15 percent of the jobs advertised. (This represents a very small number!)

- Most people get their jobs through personal and professional contacts they have already cultivated.

133

- If you don't know how to find jobs before they are listed, you are at the back of the line of people who do know how.

- Active searching exposes you to a lot more possibilities and enables you to get a better job and get it faster — it's a numbers game.

- Taking the time to research shows you not only where to look, but where *not* to look. This can save you a lot of time, frustration, and rejection down the line.

2. Use a career counselor — that's what they're there for.

Career counselors really do have a lot to offer. They have made it their business to learn things you don't have time to find out for yourself. A good guide can cut your learning curve in half and help you assess the future of your work life, customize your job search, and give you something you probably can't find in books — the personal touch. Make sure you find the right one for you — someone who takes time to get to know you and build rapport with you, provides solid assessment tools, and has the right experience and credentials.

You may wish to interview a few counselors to get the feel and breadth of their practice, and to determine if you would like working with one of them. Some of the questions you might ask are:

- How long have you been in business?

- What percentage of your clients are successful?

- What are the components of your career development process?

- What will I learn about job hunting?

- How do you structure your counseling sessions?

- How long will it take for me to learn this process?

- What will your assessment tools help me discover about myself?

- What would be your expectations of me as a client?

The first and best way to find a career counselor is by referral from people who personally recommend the person. Just as with finding a family physician, you don't want to open the phone book, close your eyes, and point. If you don't know anyone with a recommendation, call the local university — either the counseling department or the career center — and ask for resources.

The more enlightened companies don't just send employees packing without forewarning and without help. They provide career development services and their own career counselors for those about to be let go, which get them started in the right direction. In addition, they may have a lending library of reference books so that people can do their own research.

Whether or not a counselor is successful is often up to the client. When you walk into her office you don't just drop your problems into her lap and tell her to take care of them. "Let me know when you've found me a dream job." This is in every way a collaborative effort. Without your active involvement, she cannot help you. You have to ask informed questions and then act on her advice.

3. Be prepared for opportunities.

Let's say a job recruiter was given your name by an old colleague. Your phone rings one afternoon, and he asks you to mail him your resume right away. Is yours comprehensive? Does it sell you? The art of writing resumes changes just as styles of literature change. Is yours up-to-date?

Suppose you're a graphic designer, and you meet someone who is about to start up a new magazine. You're both intelligent people. It's a lively conversation, and you both hit it off. At the end, she mentions that she and her partners are just now interviewing arts and design people, and it might be a good idea if you dropped by their new offices next week to show them your portfolio. Is yours ready? Does it have a professional veneer? Does it represent your best, most current work, or is it dated?

To use a corny phrase, when opportunity knocks, make sure you're ready to answer the door. Not only will you not have to sit by and watch a golden opportunity disappear before your eyes because you're still scrambling to prepare, but you'll make a much better impression on a future employer if you can respond to a request with immediacy.

The resume, of course, is the minimum you need to have in a state of readiness. It must be well-thought-out, neat, expertly written, succinct, and all-inclusive. And don't forget to check little things like spelling and typos. If you are applying for a job as a nurse, you don't want the word *hospital* spelled "hopsital." You are applying for a position in which it is assumed you are educated, so you don't want to create the illusion that you aren't.

For those who have not pinpointed exactly the kind of job they are looking for — that is to say, they have a number of general skills, and there are various types of positions that would fit those skills — it is important to have more than one resume ready. Resumes today have to be sculpted towards exactly the job you want to be considered for. If you would like a job as a secretary but you could also be a receptionist, you would stress different assets about yourself in each resume. In one, you might emphasize experience that has provided you with social skills for dealing with the public. In the other, you might emphasize job experience that improved your computer and research skills.

Generally speaking, a resume is a brief statement that should describe the type of job you are looking for, your level of education, relevant past achievements, outstanding skills, and how you can be reached. Sometimes, at the end, it is a good idea to list a few of your outside interests and hobbies so that potential employers can see what a well-rounded person you are. Also, be sure to record any awards or citations you may have received.

One other thing you may want to keep in mind is to be prepared for unexpected opportunities. If you are going someplace where you may potentially encounter important contacts, make sure you dress for the role. It could be the wedding of a colleague or a casual lunch with old friends in the same profession as you. Whatever the social setting, if you are job hunting and there is any chance of a professional encounter that could help you, it is in your best interest to make a good impression right then while you can. You may not get another chance. You do not want to be seen with ketchup stains on your shirt or wearing shorts and a T-shirt by a person whom you wish to be considering you for fifty thousand a year. In all case scenarios, be prepared.

4. Investigate the norms and values of the organizations at which you might like to work.

Companies, in a way, are like people. They have a certain set of expectations about how they expect their people to interact in the workplace. They have definite ideas about the kind of values they expect employees to uphold.

If you're lucky, you know someone who knows someone who works there and that person can give you an honest appraisal. If not, through research, try to get names of people within the corporation and request an informational interview. This is an exploratory conversation, not a job interview. Remember that this person is doing you a favor, so be considerate of his time. Try to create a friendly, trusting atmosphere in which you can freely ask questions like:

- Why do you like working for this organization?

- Are you able to give your opinions openly? Does management hear and respond to them?

- Are people here happy or grumpy most of the time?

- Does your boss treat you with respect and support your efforts?

- Do you have to go through a lot of red tape if you want to make basic changes that will help employee satisfaction?

- Is management flexible to schedule changes so that employees can tend to child-care or personal needs when it is necessary?

- How good are the employee benefits?

- Does your job role change from week-to-week, or do you know what to expect?

- Do you have a suggestion box? Is there any follow-up as to what is done about the ideas that are put in it?

- What is the normal work week, forty hours or fifty to sixty hours?

- Do you have to give three months' notice to get a vacation?

- Is there a dress code?

- After a crisis that leaves people up in the air, is honest information disseminated immediately?

- Is customer service real, or is it a facade?

- Are new employees trained properly to fulfill their job roles?

We all come to an organization with our own set of values. When their values and ours are compatible, there is less inner turmoil and outer conflicts. You also need to ask questions that will give you some insight into the company's beliefs:

- Do employees here take responsibility for their own performance?

- Are staff encouraged to pitch in and help each other?

- Is there an atmosphere of respect?

- Historically, how reliable have your products been? Does management correct errors to preserve the quality of the products?

5. When you meet with an organization's representative, be prepared.

Picture this: You walk into a strange new office building and are signaled to take the elevator up to the eighteenth floor. As you hear that low hum of the elevator, are you prepared? Do you have a list of questions ready so that you walk in making a good impression? Are you feeling poised and confident or rushed and anxious?

The impression you want to create in an interview is one of intelligence, diligence, and competence. You want them to know you will be an asset to the company. Speak with a smile and ask pertinent questions. Remember to listen to the answers. Many interviewees, out of sheer nervousness, talk too much in an effort to impress the other person. If you fall into this trap, it will create the impression that you don't take instruction easily and are difficult to train.

While you are there, make notes to yourself on a pad. This does two things: it lets the employer know you are serious, and it allows you to take down information while it is still fresh. After the interview, record the name of the company, name of contact, address, and phone number. Also make a point of recording your own impressions of them. Is this a place where you are eager to work? Store all of this relevant information in a Rolodex or a file for the future. If you go on eight interviews in one week, interview numbers two and five can become a blur. Don't count on your memory to keep everything straight; count on your notes.

6. Investigate a new profession you might like to pursue.

Even if we've been relatively comfortable and successful in our present profession, sometimes we just need a change. As we grow, our interests change, and for many, those interests lead to a need to translate their passion into a source of income. For instance, someone who is a buyer for a department store may learn a lot about fabrics over the years. She may find that she has a keen eye for texture and color, and once she reaches a certain level of expertise, she might wish to switch careers and enter the textile industry. Creative people know when it is time to follow a passion and develop it into a brand new career.

We all have more than one talent. Even though you are good at your present profession, you may experience burnout or be bored with it. This means you're ready to try something new. Remember, just because you are good at a certain job doesn't mean you must do it the rest of your life. You have other talents, too. So if you want to check out the possibility of a career change, have informational interviews with people in the professions you are considering. Ask questions like:

- What is it that you like best/least about your profession?

- What characteristics or traits do people in your profession have to have?

- When do you feel most satisfied performing your work?

- How does one break into this profession?

- Are there opportunities for growth?

- Does this profession require specific credentials or educational background?

Dana

After switching my work from financial advisor to management consulting, I learned that you can have whatever you can imagine. I was determined to work in a place that used my skills, appreciated me, and matched my values. I told everyone I knew and everyone I met at networking events what I was looking for. I made calls to different organizations and asked plenty of questions so I could see what my options were. Then, one day, I was talking to someone at a management consulting firm, and we hit it off. She suggested I come in and talk with the Human Resources Director. I did, and during the next two weeks I was interviewed and hired. It had taken me six months of searching, but I found exactly the right job for me.

Networking

This bears repeating: networking is a vital part of the work world. Whether you keep the job you have or seek another job you want, you can't make it alone. Since we mostly find jobs through referrals, it is important to know as many people as you can who could potentially pave the way for you to meet your next employer.

The Fine Art of Networking

Often, we think if we go to a meeting or two and shake hands with at least three people, we are networking. Well, that may be part of the picture, but actually networking is so much more. It means keeping in ongoing contact with a large, extended group of people. They may be people with common interests, business associates, association compadres, or hobby enthusiasts. The bottom line is: Do they know someone you may want to know in the future?

Where do you meet people? Go to meetings, conferences, events, anywhere and everywhere that the kind of people who can help you hang out. Either get on committees or lead them. Active people are always more visible.

How to Stay Visible and Build a Good Image

Leave a good lasting impression with people when networking:

1. Be reciprocal — always ask "What can I do for you?"

Help people out whenever you can, because they don't forget that.

Julie

When I was a recruiter, I helped a woman who had lost her job to understand various aspects of the job market. Then, I left my job and decided to open my own business as a temporary staffing agency. Now, this same woman is president of a company and uses me exclusively to fill her openings.

2. Always remember to say thank you.

You wouldn't believe how many people forget this simple thing. A thank you note helps you stand out as someone who has manners, who knows how to act in the business world, and it places you in high regard in people's memories.

3. Don't just call people when you want their help.

It leaves a poor impression of you. Once you've met the right people, stay actively in touch in the myriad of ways offered by our electronic and written media. Go out to lunch with some key individuals from time to time. Send them a birthday card. E-mail them an informative article. Call and congratulate them if you hear they've gotten a promotion.

4. Pave the way for people you refer.

Call the person who was referred to let him know that you gave his name to a potential client, customer, or job applicant in advance of her call so she will be received quickly and warmly.

5. Become known as a good resource for referrals yourself.

Smart workers know enough people in diverse areas so that they always have someone to refer to. Make sure these are quality people who are competent and who have integrity.

Leon
Realize the value of networking. Knowing the right people, asking for help, and not being embarrassed to ask are essential. Since I've learned how to network, I could write a book on it. In fact, now the big joke is, "Ask Leon because he knows someone who knows somebody who might have a job."

Meet and build relationships with people who might influence your job future. Attend and become active in professional and community organizations. Join "leads" clubs, attend business or trade meetings, and participate in work-place activity groups, church groups, or Toastmasters.

Ricky

I was fortunate to meet a lot of people through my professional association, which recognized my work at their awards receptions for a few years. I did not realize it at the time, but I was net-working, and peers were seeing my work. Years later, when I decided to go out on my own as a consultant, people in the field knew me, and I was able to keep my independent practice very busy without ever marketing myself.

And then you can always:

- Collect business cards. Write notes on cards you receive indicating who the person is, where you met them and how to follow up with them.

- Give business cards that promote you with a few articulate sentences written on the back about who you are or what you are looking for.

- Have three standard questions memorized that you ask people, like:
  - ✧ What does your department/company do?
  - ✧ Are they looking for people with my professional abilities and experience?
  - ✧ Whom would I contact there to learn more?

- Have three standard pieces of information about yourself to offer so that you can leave a lasting impression about who you are and what your level of competency is. For instance (using your particulars of course):
  - ✧ I was able to attract new customers to my company by....
  - ✧ I saved my organization 10,000 dollars by....
  - ✧ I'm really good at....

- Consider putting your photo on both your business card and stationery, because people remember pictures more than words.

- Make sure all of your materials look sophisticated, are informative and represent you. Put your image out there as someone people will trust and want to hire.

- Keep track of the personal and business issues you discuss with people in your tracking system so you can refer to them before your next contact. People respond favorably when their conversations are remembered.

- Stay visible in a low-key, yet professional manner. Mail relevant articles of interest to your contacts on a quarterly basis or send occasional cards with an interesting quote or idea. When you are ready to job hunt, these people will remember you and accept your phone calls.

Activate the Search

First, call everyone you know and ask if they are aware of any job opportunities or if they can refer you to people who are good leads. You might feel embarrassed about asking for help, but remember, you would do this for them if they called you.

Although it is very difficult to ask for this kind of support when you feel anxious about your work life, here are some ways to make it easier and come across better:

1. Listen to your voice as you talk.

Make sure it sounds friendly and confident. If you don't feel confident, fake it. If you can't fake it, don't call that day.

2. Know exactly what you want to get out of the conversation.

Many people call and waste time trying to think of what to say while someone is hanging on the other end of the line. Instead, write down what you want to say ahead of time. Compose succinct thoughts and sentences you want to be sure to use. Make sure your questions will lead to real answers. Also, pre-think the answers you may receive from your requests so that you can respond to them with some forethought.

3. Practice your phone conversations before you call.

Simulate a phone conversation with a person you want to call. Make your opening statement, ask your questions, answer questions and close your call. Do this several times.

4. Be considerate of people you call.

They are more likely to invite you to call again if you are considerate of their time and show appreciation for efforts in your behalf. When you reach people by phone, after you greet them warmly tell them in fifteen seconds why you are calling and ask if they have five to ten minutes to talk with you or if it would be better for you to call at another time. If they're busy, don't keep them on the line. When you do talk later, stay within the agreed-upon time and be a clock-watcher. Remind them when time is almost up and reiterate that you want to honor their time needs. If they extend the time, stay on. If they don't, end the call. At the end of the conversation, thank them for their time and advice.

5. Take notes.

Have pen and paper, or preferably a contact management program on your computer, to organize your calls and conversations easily. Take notes of your conversation while on the phone. You will remember important points if you write them down while talking.

6. Follow up immediately.

Use any suggestions you felt were useful right away. Often, we put things aside and then never get to them.

7. Write a thank you note.

Expressions of appreciation are always a winner. In addition to saying thank you, offer to be of help in the future.

8. Keep this person informed of your progress.

It serves you, for it keeps your name in front of that person for future opportunities. And people like to know they have made a contribution.

9. Leave an interesting voice mail.

When you request a returned call, try to state what you want in a way that will pique their interest, or intrigue them enough to call you back.

Pick up Free Information from the Internet

There is an enormous amount of information on all aspects of the job search just waiting for you on the Internet. Try the different search engines (Yahoo, Alta Vista, and others) on the Web or find links through your online service. Just type in key words — "career," "workplace," "job," or the name of a company or industry, book titles, authors, magazines.

You will be amazed at what you discover. You will find articles from newspapers and other periodicals, and discover trends and issues in your field. Here, you will find comparative information about salaries, interviewing skills, networking and everything you need to know to get a job, start your own business, or any other endeavor you have in mind. You can even put your resume on-line. Since there are many books available telling you how to go about these searches — and you can learn this skill on-line as well — I will offer a few connections here.

As of this writing, the following are some of the better gateway sites on the Web:

What Color Is Your Parachute? (www.washingtonpost.com/parachute) is a gateway to information about job-hunting Web sites. It provides a comprehensive look at the use of the Internet for job-hunters or career-changers. It is organized according to six categories: overview sites, resume sites, job-listing sites, career counseling sites, research sites, and contact sites. It also lists the best, and the best-known sites, together with Richard Bolles's insights about what to do when these sites don't pay off for you. Richard Bolles is the author of the job-hunting book, *What Color Is Your Parachute?*

The Riley Guide (www.dbm.com/jobguide) Links to recruiters; local and international job opportunities; resources for women, minorities, and other diverse groups; resume sites; resources for specific occupations; coaching on using the Internet for career management; and more.

According to *Electronic Recruiting News*, over 2,500 Web sites offer job postings. Some companies also list positions on their Web sites. Here are a few to get you started.

Careerbuilder (www.careerbuilder.com) Offers links to sixteen specialized career sites.

149

CareerMosaic (www.careermosaic.com) Offers listings from leading corporations.

CareerWeb (www.cweb.com) Has thousands of job listings from hundreds of major companies.

JobOptions (www.joboptions.com) This is one of the largest and best-known sites.

Hot Jobs (www.hotjobs.com) Helps employers streamline their recruiting process.

JOBTRAK (www.jobtrak.com) Has more than 40,000 listings and links to 750 college campuses across the United States.

JobWeb (www.jobweb.org) Has more than 1,600 member universities and 1,600 employers.

The Monster Board (www.monster.com) Has more than 50,000 listings.

Net-Temps (www.nettemps.com) Has more than 75,000 listings.

Online Career Center (www.occ.com) Attracts leading employers.

jobEngine (www.jobengine.com) Is a job-posting and resume-search site for computer industry professions.

Continue Being an Effective Employee

Just because you're ready to move on, you think you aren't being treated well in your present job, or you are upset with larger issues in your organization, don't let your reputation slip by under-performing. Always maintain a good demeanor and stay professional. In fact, you can proactively reach out to help or improve areas where you can contribute your insight, support, and competence even if you'll only be there another two weeks. This attitude will help you maintain a good reputation long after you're gone, and you never know when you'll need it.

1. Believe in yourself and believe in others.

When people catch "downsizing fever," caused by the rampant fear of job loss, anxiety builds and self-esteem plummets. Don't take layoffs personally. They are about finances and company solvency, not about you or your skills.

Remember your capabilities and all the things you have accomplished so far. Perhaps you have had temporary setbacks before and came through them. Think back about how you held up and survived. You will again.

Once you realize that you will be just fine, help others believe in themselves, too. Lift morale by demonstrating an optimistic attitude and encouraging people to do their best. Then, you have not only supported them, but helped them build an environment that will support you, too. You will be remembered for your excellent attitude when someone is seeking your type of skills.

2. Be valuable and provide quality work.

We do not make friends or influence people when we are self-absorbed. The best way to overcome an unending interest in only ourselves is to make a point of reaching out and helping others.

Find ways to support co-workers and your organization that goes beyond your work role. You will find that it improves your own frame of mind enormously. At the same time, if you are a good employee — competent, conscientious, accountable, action-oriented, and caring toward others — you will be seen as a valuable source of strength.

Today, employers are hungry for people they can depend on to manage their own workloads successfully. When they view you as an asset, they might make sure to keep you!

3. Keep communicating, even if you don't care anymore.

Help people overcome their panic by only sharing accurate workplace news. In other words, discourage gossip. Work environments often become rumor mills of distorted information that only heightens fears. People become upset about things that are not real, and this drives down employee morale and productivity.

4. Be a problem solver.

The last thing someone needs when they think they are about to go over a cliff is another problem. Instead, contribute solutions.

- Identify the problem.
- Gather and organize data.
- Analyze the data.
- Develop a plan.
- Recommend solutions.
- Communicate ideas.
- Implement selected solutions.
- Decide on the next steps.

5. Be a good supervisor, if that's your role.

If you supervise others, you may be suffering a double dose of stress because you are not only concerned about your job, but you need to help keep up the spirits and productivity of staff who feel less secure about keeping *their* jobs. Learn how to manage others well, with the same consideration *you* would want. If you cannot do that, you might want to think about whether or not you even want to supervise. Managing people is not everyone's cup of tea. Often, people are promoted to that role for doing a good job with their technical, clinical, creative, mechanical, or other skills. But a managerial role requires solid people skills in communication, feedback, coaching and conflict management, which can be acquired either through training or through the "School of Hard Knocks." I recommend getting trained. It will save you from falling on your face.

6. Be appreciative.

Everyone needs acknowledgment. It sure lifts the spirits when we are down. Thank people in many ways. And do it with sincerity — if you overdo it, you will not be believed. Remember, people at all levels of responsibility need appreciation, from the front line employee to the CEO. There is one other benefit to being appreciative. Positive feedback regulates the seratonin system in the brain. When the seratonin level is balanced it enhances self-esteem and impulse control and your brain functions better. When we are negated, the seratonin level drops and our brains don't function as well. So a simple *well done*, at times, can literally raise people out of a depressed state.

7. Be visible.

Let influential people know who you are, what you do, and what you have accomplished.

People recommend the ones they are acquainted with, those with proven skills and good reputations, a lot more easily then they recommend people who are tucked away in a back office doing a great job that no one knows about.

SUMMARIZED POINTS

1. With the rapid changes in technology, many employers expect employees to find new jobs every two to four years or they're considered dead wood.

2. You will find it empowering to take your future into your own hands.

3. Look for new opportunities in your present organization.

4. Acquire the habit of lifelong learning.

5. Investigate new careers that attract you.

6. Prepare for your transition.

7. Learn the job search process.

8. Do volunteer work to bolster your skills.

9. Network, network, network.

10. While at your present job, be an effective employee, even if you know you'll be leaving soon.

CHAPTER SEVEN

WHAT TO DO AFTER YOU'VE LOST YOUR JOB

*"It's not what happens to us but our response
to what happens to us that hurts us."*
— Steven Covey

It cannot be over-emphasized how much in the industrialized world, people's identities are hooked into what they do for a living. If that is threatened, everything they take themselves to be is threatened. How you are seen by society, how much respect you get, what level of intelligence you are seen to have — all are tagged by what kind of job you have. If you are at a party and you tell people you are an electrical engineer, you will get one kind of reaction. If you tell them you are a piecework seamstress, you will get another kind. And if you have no job at all, you will distinctly feel the reactions whether they are spoken or not. Society pressures us to fashion an image of ourselves by dangling the carrot of importance and worth in front of us and by threatening us from behind with the stick of humiliation if we fail to measure up.

"It's embarrassing when you're used to being a highly respected professional, and then, suddenly, you lose your job. I was in a state of shock and didn't know what I was going to do. At first, I didn't tell anyone, not even my wife."

— Austin

Many people who are out of work, no matter how temporary the situation is, feel as if they are invisible. The job made them feel like somebody. It gave them a face, a sense of security. They were able to wake up every morning believing firmly in the status quo. And, of course, they knew that payday was on Friday. If you find yourself without a job, the purpose of this chapter is to show you some things you can do about your own frame of mind and about your actual situation to climb out of the hole you think you are standing in.

It's important to remember that you are one among millions of people who, at one time or another, have found themselves in this position. In fact, ask around. See if you can find a single person who has *not* been out of work, and looking and feeling badly about himself. Yet many of these people have gone on to even better jobs than they had before, and they are more satisfied with their lives. As a bonus, the whole process of reviving their depressed state of mind, revving up their energy, and taking charge of their life has caused them to mature in ways they could not have expected.

"When I got laid off, I hid inside my house because I just couldn't face people. I could no longer tell who I was. Whenever someone has asked me what I do for a living, my answer has always been the basis for who I am."
—Helen

Unfortunately, life is not just smooth sailing. Most of us have obstacles to overcome, and how we do that determines not only the quality of our character, but the quality of our very life. Anything that turns our life upside down seems catastrophic at first. What we don't realize is that the effort we make to overcome adversity reveals to us capacities and resources we never knew we had. This tale of meeting adversity head-on and prevailing is so common and so old that it is actually encapsulated in myths. Joseph Campbell, noted author and philosopher, described it as *the hero's journey.*

- There is the hero (you), who sets out on a quest. *Your search for meaningful work, and abundance.*

- Everything seems to go well enough for a while, but then you are presented with an obstacle. *You are fired, downsized or ostracized.*

- In a heroic way, you overcome the obstacle. *Through perseverance and pain, you search for and find a better job.*

The Hero's Journey through Rough Seas

- You return home a transformed person whom all the world recognizes and respects. *You return to your inner home where you now have a new understanding of yourself as well as higher self-esteem, which you project outward for the world to see.*

This progression can describe your own personal victory as you grapple with the challenges fate throws in your way so that you can arrive at a new plateau in your life.

Austin

"You Got the Ax; Now What Should You Do?"
glared a New York Times *headline in 1989. It
seemed to be written just for me. I'd just been laid
off as vice-president of marketing for a major shoe
manufacturing corporation. After nine years in this
senior position, a company consolidation knocked
me right out of action.*

*At first, I read myself the riot act. "Why didn't
you see this coming?" Then, I started questioning
myself, who I was as a professional, as a husband,
as a parent and as a human being. Facing my
peers was really hard because I had mentored
some of them, and they were doing better than I
was. My shame almost consumed me. You know, I
grew up hearing that men are not supposed to cry,
but I almost did.*

*Then, I began to go through a process of deep
introspection. Sometimes, I would go sit in church
just to find some peace of mind. Other times, I
would just drive up in the hills near where I live
and be alone with nature. Over time, I realized that
I really did enjoy my profession, and I wanted to
continue doing it. But corporations weren't hiring
at the moment, so I decided to start my own business. Fortunately, people did not hold my layoff
against me. In fact, they readily hired me for consulting projects when I let them know I was ready
to work.*

Downsizing Can Be a Gift

That is why I say that losing your job can be a gift in disguise. Often, we need a jarring shove out of our comfort zones, those places in life and work that we can easily nestle into and never attempt to leave. There may be no troubling challenges, no problems, and no new decisions to be made, but there is also no personal growth, no excitement, no new ideas or skills, and no way to activate our capabilities. You don't find out the stuff you are made of when you stay with the familiar.

Imagine walking in the desert. The sand is blowing, the heat is stifling, there is only enough water to extinguish your thirst, but not enough to set up a home or grow crops. Yet, you stay anyway because you "know the desert." Does this make sense? I realize this example is extreme, but the point is important. As long as we don't take the risk to step out of the familiar, we will continue wandering around the featureless landscape we are used to.

When you get laid off completely against your will, life is thrusting you into a strange new environment. To shift to another metaphor, you will either sink or swim. Most people would rather do anything than sink, so they will dig deep inside of themselves and learn to swim. And then they will feel invigorated by the effort. They will find that they actually like using these new swimming muscles. In time, they come to appreciate the fact that they were thrown into the water without a life preserver because it got them to use and develop these muscles they never knew they had.

"I learned that comfort in a job is not always advantageous to personal growth and that change is important to the evolution of the spiritual side of yourself. Staying in the same job because it's easier than changing, leaves you with emptiness. It depends on your goals. I had bigger things to learn in life, but I didn't realize it until after I got my pink slip."

— Paula

The Real Payoff

The idea that downsizing ends a person's career, financial stability and work future appears to be a myth. A nation-wide survey conducted by Interim Services, Inc. shows that:

- Sixty-two percent of those who lost or left a job because of downsizing feel that they are now *better off professionally* than they used to be.

- More than four out of ten (44 percent) employed adults who lost a job due to down-sizing view the experience as having *opened new opportunities.*

- More than half (54 percent) say they can *balance their work and personal lives better now.*

Sondra

I just couldn't believe it when they told me I was laid off. I had been at that place a long time, and I was really comfortable with my job. When I lost it, I decided that instead of jumping into another job right away, I would take time to travel to the places I've always wanted to see. I took a trip to Europe, Canada and the northeast coast of the United States. When I returned home, some-one I used to work with called me and told me about a job at her company. I went on an interview and got it. So this great job as administrative assistant to the president just fell in my lap.

Sometimes you need to get pushed out the door to see what you can do. At the time that it happens, it is scary to let go, but in the end it is also energizing. What I found was that if I approached it as an opportunity, it was one.

Where to Use Your Talents

If you are living in America, you are working in one of the most prosperous countries in the world. Opportunities abound. New companies are springing up everywhere, making more jobs available all the time. And with the growing international economy, we have a bigger sandbox to play in than in any previous decade or era. You just have to find your niche.

Since good employees — ones who are conscientious and productive, who are problem solvers and work well with others — are hard to find, more options are open to them. According to *U.S. News and World Report*, in June 1997, "There were 121.8 million jobs in America — more than ever before. The national unemployment rate was 4.8 percent, the lowest in twenty-three years. White-collar workers, professionals, and workers in skilled trades were also finding good salaried positions."

Schools, both public and private, seminar groups and other educational programs are continually helping people upgrade their present skills or acquire new ones to meet job market demands. As the world economy grows, so do the range of possibilities.

What to Do as You Prepare for Your Next Move

So, now that you know you're sitting pretty, how do you make your next move? It is remarkably easier to do this if your head and heart are functioning together. People who are out of work go through intense emotional turmoil. In an effort to distance themselves from the discomfort, they cut off from their feelings. The rationale behind it is that their fear and shame will only hold them back. In reality, *not* facing your feelings will hold you back more. Emotions that are kept in the shadows exert a hidden influence, and often undermine our resolve and confidence when we are least expecting it. To be truly strong, we need to acknowledge our feelings and learn how to work through them. On the other hand, we need to act practically and realistically in order to get back on our feet. Here are some suggestions to help.

1. Try not to panic.

Panic causes a person to lose perspective. It puts us in exactly the wrong frame of mind for making decisions and taking appropriate actions. We just want to run, and it is usually in the wrong direction. Instead of reality determining our direction, fear determines it.

So first, we need to calm our fears so we will be ready to handle whatever comes along. One way to diffuse your panic is with hard facts. Even in dire circumstances most people manage to find a myriad of ways to keep a roof over their head, their car running, and their children in school. In short, they get by. All the while, they do what it takes to find their next job. The important thing is to search for ways to calm you down, and allay your worst fears and most catastrophic expectations.

Sandy

I believe that whatever occurs in life, there is a reason for it. It may be that I need to learn something new, unlearn bad habits, or just shift and broaden my thinking. Even though I wish that some of the golden lessons of the past hadn't needed to be gained at the expense of so much pain and frustration, I still wouldn't give them up for anything. Just having that kind of faith gives me comfort and hope to hang in there no matter what happens.

One thing that can help is learning to have faith. A belief system that supports you in times of crisis can make a big difference.

2. Do a reality check.

What is it about the human mind that makes it jump to the worst conclusion, and makes it picture the most catastrophic scenario when faced with bad news? The logical side of our brain, which would quickly toss these panicky thoughts out the window, seems to go out of commission just when we need it. Our emotional side takes over, and the intensity gets notched up ten points. When this happens, we need to discipline ourselves and conduct a reality check so we can stay grounded.

a. Remind yourself that you are a capable person.

Make a list of past successes so you can see in black and white you are not the loser you are accusing yourself of being. Just because you lost a job does not mean you have lost your natural abilities or your talents. Tape the list to the wall in a prominent place to keep yourself aware of all that you have done before and can do.

b. Start looking for the diamond in the silt.

Since things are up in the air anyway, this may be the perfect time to make some changes. Perhaps there is a new company springing up that sounds exciting, and you would like to take a chance on it. Or a new industry is opening up where you could apply your skills in challenging and innovative ways. Start picturing these scenarios as real and possible.

c. Begin to remind yourself of who you really are at your core.

You may feel you are invisible within this culture if you are out of work, but don't become invisible to yourself.

It is important to maintain a strong sense of your own identity, both for your own peace of mind and because it will serve you well to project that when you go on a job interview.

d. Get some perspective on how long it takes to find another job.

There is no point in setting yourself up for disappointment. If you've got it wedged into your brain that you should have a new job within five working days, and then that doesn't materialize, you are going to be left disappointed and scared about your future. But what if it typically takes three months to find a new job in your field? Then you have scared yourself for nothing. Develop a realistic perspective that lets you know what the norm is and gives you a context in which to plan your moves.

e. Remember other tough times in your life.

Perhaps you were in the depths of despair, or angry over an injustice, or terrified that your whole life would come tumbling down around your ankles. Think back to the very worst day. It was awful. You were miserable. Then came the second day and you were still pretty miserable, but there was a five-minute window of time when you felt okay. On the third day, it was ten minutes. As time went by, and you moved on in your life, the whole thing became nothing but one big unhappy memory. Somehow you overcame it all. It may have taken time, but you did it. If you conquered your problems then, you will do it today.

3. Guard against depression.

Depression is a drastic downswing in mood. It is characterized by feelings of extreme dejection and hopelessness. It injects us with an attitude of defeatism, and we cannot help but begin to view the future as bleak. Depressed people negate everything that happens to them, even if it is good. Within that frame of mind, it is almost impossible to spot and utilize a good opportunity when it comes along.

When you haven't got a reliable job to go to, it is easy to spiral downward into a deep depression. Some physical and psychological symptoms are:

- self-flagellation
- unrealistic worries
- crying fits
- guilt
- lethargy
- forgetfulness
- helplessness

- feelings of worthlessness
- lack of motivation
- poor or over-active appetite
- inability to concentrate
- loss of interest
- insomnia

4. Stay physically healthy.

You are more vulnerable to illness when absorbed by pessimistic thoughts about your future or bitterness about the past. More than ever, you need to eat, exercise, and rest properly. You also need to be careful that you don't let destructive behaviors immobilize you.

a. Don't give in to drugs or alcohol.

One of the worst things you can do to yourself is become numb to life from drugs or alcohol. These intoxicants will cloud your thinking processes and make you ineffective and unrealistic. As a result, you may not take the actions needed to find the right job. Your decision-making abilities will be impeded, and you might take the wrong job. Or, you might make an unfitting comment, behave inappropriately or otherwise embarrass yourself in front of others and bury your chances of getting any job at all.

b. Don't binge on comfort foods.

Many of us use food as a friend to cover up unhappiness, emptiness, or anxiety. Or we use it as a support when we feel like our lives are reeling out of control. The tendency is to either over-eat or to go in for comfort foods, those with a lot of sugar, fat, and calories. I do not need to tell you that these foods are a body explosion waiting to happen.

The particular problem with this, when you are in-between jobs, is that number one, appearances count, and number two, your self-esteem needs to be maintained. For most of us, when we balloon up over our normal weight, it is hard to look at ourselves in the mirror without cringing. We feel awkward because our clothes don't fit. There is no question that in some cultures weight directly affects self-esteem. The last thing you want when you are out there selling your virtues to others is to have nagging doubts about your waistline. In addition, like it or not, an attractive appearance does matter for many jobs, especially anything in the public eye. So not only is your subjective view of yourself affected by weight gain from overeating, but so is the objective view of others.

c. Don't take up old addictions.

At this time, your resolve may be in a weakened state, and you may allow yourself to be coaxed back into an old addiction, like smoking or gambling. Don't! You will just lower your chances of success. One of the least-talked-about effects of addictions is that they weaken the will. Drugs and alcohol are the worst offenders, but on some level, all addictions do it. So at just the time when you need to summon all of your will, which comprises determination, persistence, strength, and purpose, you are taking in substances that are directly wearing down your will and working against your own best interests.

5. Develop a healthy mental attitude about losing your job.

You have not committed a crime, and you have nothing to be ashamed of. You have simply joined the ranks of the unemployed like many before you. Yes, it is embarrassing. Yes, it is uncomfortable. I am not minimizing how you feel about it. What I am saying is, go through whatever emotional cleansing you need to, to flush it all out of your system, and then get on with your life.

You'll feel a lot better if you can adopt the right frame of mind. Your perspective will influence the course you chart for your future. For instance, when something goes wrong in life, if you can accept that there are valuable lessons for you to learn, then you can use the lemons to make lemonade.

"During the first six months of unemployment, I would wake up at three in the morning in a state of total panic. 'What are you going to do?' 'How are you going to pay your bills?'"

— Mary Jane

6. Assess your financial situation.

I've been at minus zero and come out of it. So can you. To get by in the interim, you need to do two things: use the resources available to you and find ways to lower your expenses.

a. Use your resources.

- Look into what monetary resources there are to support you for the next six months or so. How much money must you have to get by?

- Make a budget.

- For those of you who are fortunate enough to have severance pay, divide it into monthly increments and dole it out to yourself over time.

- Learn about other benefits you may continue to get from your former employer.

- Use 401(k)s and investment program money as emergency money if you need it. Remember, it's not only hurricanes and tsunamis that classify as emergencies. If you really need the money, it also falls under that category.

- Find alternative ways to make money. Consulting on the side will provide much-needed cash and will keep your hand in the game. Odd jobs can exercise skills you don't usually get to employ and they can be interesting and fun.

b. Lower expenses.

- Lower food costs by eliminating restaurant eating and expensive shortcuts like fast foods and frozen meals. Make your own ready-to-go meals by cooking large quantities and freezing them.

- Reduce entertainment expenses. There are many low-cost and even free things to do out there. For instance, invite people over for a potluck dinner and play games or watch a video. Attend programs in local parks and community centers.

- Trade services with others. For example, if you are good on the computer and you need someone who is good designing brochures, you have barter potential. Many people today are getting what they need this way.

- Put a hold on frivolous spending for things you would like but don't need. Curtail visits to stores that tempt you into buying luxury items.

- Seed a fund with a set amount of money to reward yourself for good behavior. Then go out and spend it all. This will give you something to look forward to.

c. File for unemployment.

Take advantage of a government resource designed to support you. If you have been employed by a company, they have, by law, contributed a certain amount of money to the government to support people who lose jobs. Often, this income helps people get through. Although different states govern their process of providing aid independently, they have some things in common:

- Your weekly check, called the Weekly Benefit Award (WBA), and the total amount in your claim, called your Maximum Benefit Award (MBA), are both based on the amount you earned in the base period of your claim.

- A claim remains on file for one year. This is called the benefit year. In this year, weekly benefits may be paid for twenty-six weeks or until you have received half of your base period wages, whichever is less.

- Normally, you cannot file another claim until the benefit year of the first claim ends, even though you have received all your benefits and are still unemployed.

7. Get personal support.

This is not an easy time for you. Many people think they have to be completely independent spirits when times get rough. But why should you? As long as you are fully using all your own internal resources, you know you are personally doing everything that *you* can do alone. Now it's time to seek support from others.

a. Look to your family.

Get your family together for a meeting once you have fully assessed the situation, you know how to present the facts, and you know what you need to ask from them. Be specific. Be polite, but direct. Now is not the time to mince your words. Your family cares about you, and even if it is not obvious to you at first, they want to support you. Your job is to orchestrate it so that they do it in a healthy, beneficial way that you have thought about ahead of time — a way that meets your own specific emotional needs. At the same time, don't ask for them to do the things that would weaken your personal initiative. Too much dependency is not good, either.

Janice

After I lost my job, my family was always asking the same questions when they got home from work at the end of the day. "Have you found a job yet?" Or, "How come you stayed home today and didn't go on any interviews?" They thought their prodding was helpful, but all it was doing was undermining my confidence. What they didn't understand was that I didn't want to rush into another job. I know that's the family tradition, but I had given it a lot of deep thought, and I realized that it was a time in my life when I wanted to consciously choose how I earned my living so that it had some meaning to me. Even if I made less money, at least I would be spending eight to ten hours a day doing something worthwhile instead *of adding and subtracting numbers at a tax return company as I had been.*

So I called a family meeting. I thanked everyone for all their concern first. Then I told them that I was in a time of transition, that I was making a career change, and that I needed time to think it through carefully. Going on endless job interviews for another position as a numbers cruncher was not in line with that goal. Once they fully understood the situation, they had faith in what I was attempting to do. They understood that I needed their support and understanding, not their advice. From that point on, when they came home from work, they asked me how I was doing emotionally and reassured me constantly that I could pull it off.

b. Don't accept pity get-togethers.

Be aware of falling into the pit of going to a lot of sympathy lunches with contacts who feel sorry for you. On the other hand, don't retreat either. You need to maintain a strong and positive image of yourself when you are out looking for a job. Don't let it look as if it has somehow affected your character and you are not the same valuable person you were when you had a job. So, go to lunch. Be visible. Thank people for their kindness. But make sure they know you don't want sympathy. What you want and expect is a good job because you deserve it. Ask them for suggestions and contacts. This is not the place to ask for emotional support, but professional support.

c. Get together with others in the same situation as you.

No one has more understanding about your predicament than others who have also lost jobs. They have experienced the same shock, fear, and sense of loss. They are also facing similar challenges about how to conduct a job search, how to alleviate their panic, how to get support, how to get by. Find out through local unemployment centers and community groups if such support groups already exist. If not, start one. There are probably hundreds of other people living in your vicinity who are sitting around wishing for the same thing, yet not knowing what to do about it. Also talk to people who have graduated to better jobs, incomes, or lifestyles. It is always wise, while you are still at base camp, to hang out with people who have already climbed the mountain and reached the summit.

8. Plan your next steps.

When you go from the structure of a nine-to-five job to no set schedule at all, you need to pick up a few tools:

- Use time management skills.

- Stay focused on the results you are looking for.

- Keep up your spirits and stay self-motivated.

Austin

I think it is terribly important to develop a daily schedule and stick to it. If the alarm clock isn't going off at six, there is a tendency in the morning to stay in bed longer, not shave, and sit around the kitchen table drinking coffee. As soon as I saw myself doing this, I snapped out of it. You don't want to act like a person who is out of work, who is in trouble emotionally, and all the rest. You need to deal with it, but not let it show when you are out looking for a job.

- Set up a space at home to conduct your job search and personal growth materials. Make sure that children, pets, and other mischief-makers can't get into them.

- Keep as many other things in your life organized as you can. Any kind of chaos can affect your frame of mind.

- Develop a daily schedule so you don't waste time.

- Plan your job search/life search.

Guard against Fall-Out Behaviors

1. Avoid bitterness and backbiting.

It is so destructive. What's done is done. Don't increase the hostility by keeping it alive in your mind. It will only come back around and hit you in the head when you are least expecting it. This means you cannot give in to the temptation to berate your former employer or anyone else you believe is at fault. It may feel satisfying at the time to vent your anger, and frustration, and sense of being wronged, but this kind of thing only damages your reputation and makes you look petty. Let it go so you can move on.

2. Learn from your mistakes.

Mistakes are meant to be learning aids, not just another thing to beat yourself up with. They teach us what *not* to do. The mistakes we pay attention to are the ones we don't have to go on repeating. (Read "Autobiography in Five Short Chapters" on page 35.)

3. Don't jump at the wrong job too soon.

When fear governs, we do crazy things, like snapping up the wrong job because our fear makes us believe that any job is better than no job at all. Don't jump before you know where you will land, or you might find yourself in the same position you were in before: doing something you don't like, in a soulless environment, with unpleasant people who don't know how to treat each other.

If you jump too soon, you could also find yourself out of a job again within months because you didn't research the company. But this time, you may end up with more anger and fear and less money than before.

Margaret

I was so desperate to leave my last employer that I leapt at a sales job with a local magazine without looking into it at all. In my interview, I was told that my territory had five thousand potential customers and that my commissions could net me an extra ten thousand dollars a month. Unfortunately, once I was on board, I found out they had stretched the truth considerably. For one thing, my territory turned out to be much smaller than they had indicated. Consequently, the commission possibilities dropped to two thousand dollars a month. Had I done my homework and checked the place out, I might have learned all that before it was too late.

4. Don't slow down your job search just because you have a few possible opportunities.

Job hunting is no fun. We can all agree on that. Most of us want to stop the process the first chance we get. This is not a good idea. Until you are positive the position has been awarded to you, you need to keep your search strategy in gear.

Actually, the time you feel good because the fish seem to be biting is exactly when you should be out there conducting more interviews, even if you are "certain" you are about to be hired somewhere. It is at this time that we are our best at selling ourselves. So go on as many interviews as possible because you will make your best impression. You never know, you might find something even better or make contacts for future jobs.

Malie

I had been out of work for three months. After my final interviews with two companies, which I felt sure would both offer me jobs, I was frankly relieved because I was so sick of looking. One company praised my qualifications and told me they would let me know that Friday. The other company said I would hear from them the following Monday. Now, in my mind, all I had to do was decide which company's offer to accept.

Friday came, no call. Monday came, no call. Now, a little concerned, I attempted to reach both interviewers by phone. Neither one returned my calls. After a few days, I got the standard thank you letter from both stating that although I had been one of the top candidates, they had selected someone else. I couldn't believe it.

You also need to stay on the interview circuit until you have literally put your Rolodex on your new desk and your calendar on the wall, because it is possible to be hired, and before your first day at work the conditions there change. In organizations these days, there are constant regrouping strategies taking place. Someone new can take over the department that hired you and develop new parameters for the job. Suddenly, you're a square peg in a round hole, and they don't need you. A budget could get cut, which would eliminate the position you are being hired for. A friend of the new manager may be offered the job and displace you. These things might not be fair, but they do happen.

Also, don't make assumptions that you got the job, even if your interviewer smiles winningly, lets you do most of the talking, eagerly answers all your questions, and makes encouraging remarks. That is her job. She is supposed to make potential employees feel warm and welcome. That doesn't mean you won the prize. She will conduct herself in the same way with the other fifty people she interviews. She will tell them all that the job will be awarded by a certain date and they will be informed of their status.

As you can see from this chapter, you have to keep alert on a number of different fronts in order to take care of yourself and present the best possible picture of yourself to the world at large. One of the purposes of this book is to show you how many ways there are to do this. You have also been reading about people in the same position as you are. Some learned the hard way, and some learned an easier way. By applying the information presented, you can be one of the people in the second group.

SUMMARIZED POINTS

1. People who have lost or left a job are often better off professionally now than they used to be.

2. Today's job market is looking for people who are conscientious, productive problem solvers, and work well with others.

3. Sometimes, we need a jarring shove out of our comfort zones to move us to a better future.

4. Your mind is a great asset. Make sure you stay emotionally strong when faced with being thrown out of work.

5. Have faith in yourself.

6. Don't take job downsizing personally.

7. Remember, you are the hero on your hero's journey.

8. Ask yourself, "What is the worst thing that can happen?"

9. Staying in the same job because it's easier leaves you in the middle of nowhere.

10. Plan what to do if you think you are about to lose a job.

CHAPTER EIGHT

MANAGING CHANGE

*"We are living in the time of the parenthesis,
the time between eras. Those who are willing
to handle the ambiguity of this in-between
period and to anticipate the new era will be
a quantum leap ahead of those who hold on
to the past."*

— *John Naisbitt*

I won't even start this chapter with all the clichés about how fast everything is changing these days. We all know that change has been one of the in-your-face themes of working people in the 1990s. And yet no matter how much is written about change, human beings still struggle with making any sort of profound transition in life. It isn't any easier for us than it was for the cave man when the ice age occurred, when the air began to have a distinct chill in it, and he had to figure out how to skin animals and wrap himself up for warmth. These days, a lot of us still feel like we're out in the cold and we're wondering what to do about it.

There are two basic kinds of change: that which we choose and that which we feel has been chosen for us. The overwhelming belief is that number one is easier, but this is not necessarily true. People who have purposely left one job for another can sometimes find it surprisingly difficult to make the transition, mainly because they didn't realize it was going to be difficult. They thought they understood themselves: where they were going, how they were going to get there, and how they would feel once they did get there. So when they found themselves floundering, they thought there was something wrong with them because they couldn't cope. Strangely enough, how difficult transition periods are doesn't have as much to do with whether or not you initiated the change as it does with how prepared you are for its stages.

The aim of this chapter is to show you the three stages that occur when going through a change and tell you what you can do to help yourself at each stage.

- **Stage One:** Your building gets dynamited
  (*you lose or leave your job*)

- **Stage Two:** You are left standing in the rubble
  (*you are between jobs*)

- **Stage Three:** You find a new building to work in
  (*you have new work*)

> *"Any real change implies the break-up of the world as one has always known it, the loss of all that gave one identity, the end of safety. And at such a moment, unable to see and not daring to imagine what the future will now bring forth, one clings to what one knew, or thought one knew; to what one possessed or dreamed that one possessed. Yet it is only when man is able, without bitterness or self-pity, to surrender a dream he has long cherished, or a privilege he has long possessed, that he is set free — that he has set himself free — for higher dreams, for greater privileges."*
> — *James Baldwin*

Stage One: Your Building Gets Dynamited

You knew the dynamite charges were being set, you were given your notice months ago, you and all the others were cleaning out your desks, preparing to exit the building. Yet no matter how prepared you were, when it was all over, the detonation was still a shock, especially if you had been working there for a long time or you had truly invested your creative energy in the place.

These are three practical things you can do to offset the jolt:

1. Ask yourself how you feel.

This is important because if you are secretly experiencing a great deal of nervous fear but you don't want to acknowledge it or take the time to deal with it, it will creep up on you in odd and destructive ways. It can cause you to make rash decisions just to make *some* decisions. It can cause you to hide out because you don't want to face anyone. Some people even cover up fear with anger, and they become belligerent exactly when they should be making friends. If you're feeling all right, that's great. But if you aren't, real strength involves facing your true feelings unflinchingly. Accepting them as normal and handling them with kindness lets you move on.

2. While acknowledging that you can't forecast everything, try to name the immediate changes you see coming up.

Stay as objective as you can and beware of over-stating the problems. What you are attempting to do is take an accurate snapshot of your situation.

If you haven't got a new job yet, you will have a lot of free time all of a sudden. That's a big change from waking up to an alarm clock, snarfing down your breakfast, and getting out of the house by seven. There will also be the drop in income. Or you might find yourself around your kids a lot more than you're used to. Note the big things and even the very smallest things because sometimes the small things are bigger than you think.

3. Make a list of the positives.

Even if you are terrified and never in a million years would have asked to be put out of your job, there is always an up side. Bad changes produce good side effects, too. You need to deliberately remind yourself of these in a list because, in the frame of mind you're in, they probably won't be popping up on their own. Think back to other changes you've gone through that have improved your life, such as when you left home at eighteen to go away to college. It made you strong and independent. Or, when you left another job years ago, and the next job you found was so much better.

Ruth

At first, I really put myself down. I thought, if they laid me off, it must be because they think I'm incompetent. I'm such a perfectionist, so any idea that someone would see me as incompetent really hurt. When I think of how I felt then, and how happy I am now, I realize that my layoff was a huge event that encompassed a lot of people. Nobody had targeted me personally. Sure, I lost my job, but in the long run, I benefited from it, for now I'm doing work I enjoy even more. And, I know I'm good at it.

Once you feel you have a pretty objective picture in front of you of how you are doing and what you are facing, you can find ways to ease yourself through this ending of a chapter of your life.

1. Be good to yourself.

As we have said in previous chapters, if you do not have another job lined up, conduct a proactive search. However, don't forget to reward and soothe yourself every day. If a good friend were in this situation, wouldn't you ask what you could do to help him feel better — perhaps take him to a ball game or to lunch? You can do the same for yourself.

*"Change can be a force to be feared
or an opportunity to be seized.
The choice is in our hands."*
—*Warren Schmidt, Ph.D.*

2. Take catastrophic fears by the horns.

We have talked about these before, but they're so important to recognize, they're worth bringing up again. These fears are the ones that fuel anxiety and cause the heart and mind to race out of control. Catastrophic fears are slippery little devils. Very often, they're in the background of our minds whispering fiendish threats, and we do not recognize what is being whispered. All we know is that we keep waking up at three in the morning in a cold sweat. Or we do recognize the threats, but somehow they sound so realistic we cannot help but take them seriously.

To see how unrealistic catastrophic fears are, you need to write them down. Be brutally honest, even if the fears seem silly. One forty-year-old, unemployed man was afraid his mother was going to come over and scold him and send him to his room without meals. A woman was afraid her pastor wouldn't let her come to church anymore because she was such a bad person for being fired from her job. Of course, both of these people, when they saw these thoughts in black and white, had to smile at how unlikely it was that these events would take place. If you look closely, you can see that they were both haunted by the thought of disapproval from someone in authority. People who do this exercise find that almost all their fears are shame-based: "We're out of a job. That means we've done something wrong, and we will be judged for it, and there will be bad luck all around." You don't need this kind of thinking undermining your self-confidence.

When someone is out of a job and doesn't know what is going to happen next, it is natural for negative emotions to come up, like shame, fear, and loss. As long as you hide from these feelings, you actually feed them energy. The only way to let go and accept the loss of your job is to get in touch with all the aspects of what the loss means to you and acknowledge whatever feelings come up.

3. Check up on your self-image.

Another thing that people fail to pay attention to when they've just lost their jobs is the effect it has had on their self-image. Everyone knows that a man's self-image is tied up with the kind of work he does. But these days, a woman's identity is becoming more linked with her career and less on her role as child-bearer than it ever did in times past. Whether you are a man or a woman, how you bring in money, what level of expertise you are at, defines your sense of value in this society.

Even if you know you'll have another job soon, the effect of losing this one may have put a big dent in your image of yourself as a responsible, competent person. You might even have a distinct picture of what an unemployed person looks like — unkempt, unshaven, slumped over, depressed. (Watch out if you find yourself checking the full-length mirror to see if you're beginning to look like this.) As with catastrophic fears, it is important to identify the hidden messages, impressions, and beliefs that exert power over your mood and outlook. Then counter them with powerful, positive self-talk.

4. Speak to friends whom you know to be sensible, grounded people.

Sometimes, when a person is caught up in runaway anxiety, she is actually drawn to someone who is going to commiserate with her about how bad it all is. This will not help. The last thing you need is someone to help convince you that your panic is grounded in reality. Talk to people who have a good head on their shoulders, who know how to listen but won't necessarily agree with everything you say. They are there to bring down your anxiety level, not to tell you you're right no matter how over-the-top your anxiety is. If you can find someone to talk to who has been through losing a job and come out well on the other end, all the better.

> "Then you leave, and it is all over — no pager, no voice mail, no e-mail.... And, they get along without you."
> — Rob

5. Let yourself grieve.

For some, the loss of a job can be almost as devastating as the loss of a loved one, and they will go through the same stages of grief.

Anger — "This isn't fair! Why is this happening to me?"

Bargaining — "If I come up with a plan to save them money, they'll take me back."

Anxiety — "I've never been in this position before. I could end up bankrupt and lose my house."

Sadness — "I worked with those people for years. They were like family to me. I really miss them."

Disorientation — "I have all these people to contact in different companies, but I don't know where to start. I was good at my job, but I don't know how to search for a new one."

Depression — "Look at the statistics. I'm out there competing with hundreds of other applicants for every job I hear about. No one is going to even notice me. I feel more hopeless every day."

Letting Go and Moving On

Moving through life is like swinging across a series of trapeze bars. You swing on one bar as another swings toward you. By letting go of the one you are on, your hands are free to grab onto the other. But, if you don't let go, you end up hanging there motionless and stuck. That describes how I was handling my life."

— Faith

Some of these stages may be more frightening to you than others. As tempting as it is, you cannot skip over the worst ones to get to the easier ones. Grieving isn't for sissies. It is a necessary emotional undertaking. Until you grieve and let go of the old, you cannot begin anew.

6. Conduct a ritual.

This may seem like New Age hocus pocus to you, but actually, people have been performing rituals to signify endings and beginnings for centuries. It fills a psychological need to honor where you have been, and what you've accomplished.

Stage Two: Standing in the Rubble

One good thing about the building blowing up was that it was a definite event. One day you were working, and the next day you weren't. There is a certain clarity to that. The aftermath is more nebulous, and the psychological effects are often harder to counteract. The "rubble period" is usually a long, drawn-out stage of uncertainty. For many people, this is much harder to bear than the building's blowing up. Waking up in the morning to a day that hasn't been structured for you can feel like free-fall. People have told me that during this period, they have a recurring dream in which they trip and fall into a bottomless well. They fall and fall into the darkness, but they never hit bottom. It is our natural tendency to want the ground beneath our feet to be firm. We want to know what is going to happen next. We can't stand things up in the air.

And yet, that is exactly what this period is about: uncertainty. The question then becomes: "How well can you tolerate uncertainty?" If you are like most, you're going to face a certain level of despondency, and depression, impatience, and frustration. In this state, you won't be hopping out of bed in the morning shouting, "Oh boy! I can't wait to get started." Even if you already set up exactly how you're going to conduct your job search, you may still be disoriented. "It's eleven o'clock on a Monday morning, and I'm sitting at my kitchen table? This doesn't seem right."

Often during this period, old flaws and uncertainties can surface that have previously been kept at bay by the fact that you were working and functioning well. I know a woman who held the same job in product testing for twelve years. When she went into it, she was thirty-two; when she left, she was forty-four. She looked older then, and that made her feel insecure about interviewing for future jobs. Or sometimes, people have been in jobs that haven't been changed much by technology. As long as they could stay put, they didn't have to challenge their backwardness around technical know-how. But once they are suddenly jetted out into the marketplace again, and they have to sell themselves to a computerized world, they become acutely aware of how behind they are.

One other thing to look for if you find yourself in this in-between state is that your reactions to others and theirs to you may go through some alterations. Wives, who have always complained that they don't get enough time with their husbands, sometimes want to eat their words when their husbands are under foot all day. They tend to look for new and ingenious ways to get them out of the house, even when they don't have a job interview to go on. Another way being out of work can put a strain on relationships is that the person who is out of a job is experiencing a lot of stress and needs extra support from his mate. If he doesn't get exactly what he needs, he feels let down. A man may want his wife to listen to him and understand what he is going through, and if she doesn't respond in perfect attunement, he will feel she doesn't care. A woman who has a lot of difficult emotions coming up might want her husband to help her process her feelings any time of day.

It helps to be aware of the fact that you will probably be extra needy during this time. While you can always ask for more than the usual amount of emotional support, this is the real world, and it is unlikely that you will get everything you ask for. Pay closer attention to how you are reacting to others while you are in the "rubble" stage. Are you being short-tempered and demanding, and driving people away from you? A little equanimity and consideration will go a long way toward easing tensions.

One way to help yourself during this difficult period is to keep reminding yourself that making a transition like this takes some time. It's not like taking off a baseball cap and putting on a rain hat. Some very deep adjustments need to be made. Try not to rush yourself.

You are now in a no-man's land. Everything that reinforced your identity in your old job is gone, and you have no idea what identity you will take on in your new job. This is a good opportunity to find out who you are without outside reinforcement. You are not the same person you were before you got your previous job. Since then, you have grown and matured. "Rubble time" doesn't have to be wasted time. In fact, if viewed properly, it can be a period of tremendous personal growth.

George

When I decided to become a lawyer, which meant going back to school for four years, it represented a major change for my wife and me. At the age of forty-five, I was giving up a considerable income. My wife and I sat down to discuss our financial picture and realized she was going to have to pick up the slack. I had never had to depend on another person for my basic needs before, and my wife had never been a sole bread-winner. This was scary for both of us. But we decided to go for it. Even though it was very stressful for us at the time, those four years were a tremendous growth experience. My wife has gained confidence in her ability to support us financially, and I learned to let go of my control around money.

It can also be a period in which you change the course of your life. You are no longer oriented so completely by your old job or company. You can have your own goals now. You have the luxury to explore what your dreams are.

If the job loss occurs when a person is in mid-life crisis, it can hit her all the harder. People in their forties and fifties often look over their life and wonder what they are doing and what it all means. While it doesn't feel at all good to ask such profound and far-reaching questions, it is actually a useful and natural process. If you meet the process head-on, you may find yourself making some of the wisest decisions of your life. Instead of letting depression and despondency make you believe this is a time of decay, you can turn things around for yourself by seeing it as a time of change and renewal.

Stage Three: You Find a New Building to Work In

The new building goes up and you walk through the front door. Everything about it is different. You feel like a kid on his first day of school.

Genuine beginnings don't really take place in an office or a hallway; they take place in the mind. You make a new beginning only after a shift in your mind occurs, and not before. If, on the first day of your new job, your mentality and attitudes are still stuck in the old job, you haven't begun your new life yet. This is another reason for giving yourself as much time as you can in the in-between period. You don't just want to slide into your new job, you want to rev up for it.

If your life up until now has kind of moved along in a groove — get off work at five, pick up the kids, stop at Pizza Hut for dinner, rent a movie, go to bed — you may want to get your creative energy going for the period of life that is now opening up to you by doing creative and active things. You can jog or finger paint, go snorkeling or take your family on an adventure. The idea is to get out of a passive mood and into an active one. To really make a fresh beginning, a promising start, you have to switch gears. What you don't want to do is sit bolt upright in bed at six in the morning on the first day of your new job and find yourself in the old passive mode.

Some of the things you will encounter as you enter your new life are inertia, clinging to the old, misgivings, apprehension, concern, and possibly regret over missed goals and unanswered challenges at the previous place of work. Beginnings often dredge up old anxieties about failure because people feel most susceptible to falling flat on their face when they don't know the terrain yet. They don't know what the rules are, and they remember how easy it was in the past to break rules they weren't aware of. At any place of work there are the stated rules, and then there are the unstated ones that reflect the culture of that particular company. If you break those the first week, you will find yourself repairing the damages for months to come.

Unfortunately, when you are the new kid on the block, everyone seems to be watching you. The angst this situation triggers can bring up memories of times past when you couldn't grasp some simple principle or piece of information, or when you blurted out the wrong thing and brought on an embarrassing silence. It seems reasonable to many that those kinds of mishaps could occur all over again now that they're starting fresh.

Here are a few points to keep in mind that will help you over the obvious stumbling blocks of your first day:

1. Be patient with yourself.

On your first day of work, you face a barrage of problems. Everyone is throwing information at you, usually assuming you know the precise category in your mind in which to file the information, even though you obviously couldn't possibly have that kind of perspective yet. People speak in incomplete sentences, don't finish their points, and use terminology you're not familiar with. They may tell you it's fine to ask questions, but everyone instinctively knows that it is not fine to ask stupid questions. The problem is, what seems stupid to the person who already knows the territory is actually a good question for someone who doesn't.

One other very common problem: Whoever is training you is probably trying to sandwich the task in with all her other tasks, so she wants to finish with you as soon as she can. She is rushing through complicated instructions and handing you big chunks of information while you're stepping onto a crowded elevator together. She tries to answer her phone the whole time you are sitting at her desk attempting to follow her description of what the chain of command is at this multi-layered corporation. It's not exactly a leisurely, nurturing, learning environment.

You're in a pickle all right. If you are insecure and you feel clumsy and stupid, don't take it personally. These are the First Day Blues. Be as patient with yourself as you can, even if those around you are giving off distinct vibrations of impatience. Know that this is a swamp you have to wade through as millions have before you.

2. Take notes.

On this day of all days you will be expected to function like a human sponge, soaking in every detail that is passed on to you. We all know that a one hundred percent retention rate isn't possible, yet so many people in authority act as if it is. I have heard stories from people who said they were expected to remember the precise wording of something on Thursday that had been told to them on Monday.

At the same time you are expected to give your full attention to your training, your attention is also doing a lot of other things. It is taking in a host of new impressions, both subtle and bold. It is trying to find out how to get you oriented to this new environment. The discipline of staying focused on your lesson with your attention being pulled in so many different ways can be likened to the problem of taking a pack of wild dogs for a walk and keeping them all going in the same direction while they all want to take off on their own.

With all this going on, don't expect yourself to remember everything tomorrow that you heard today. Taking notes will help you to get down all the pertinent information so you can refer back to it when you need to. Also, writing things down serves the same purpose as repetition; it reinforces what you heard and places it more securely in your memory. If you are embarrassed about taking notes in your little spiral pad, you can always pass off your note-taking as a favor to the other person. "This is just so I don't have to ask you to repeat yourself unnecessarily."

> *"...the willingness to move beyond*
> *received wisdom, to combine ideas from*
> *unconnected sources, to embrace change as*
> *an opportunity to test limits."*
> — *Rosabeth Moss Kanter*

3. Let go of the old and open up to the new.

One of the most common phrases managers hear with new trainees is, "At the old place we did it a different way." Not to put too fine a point on this, but it doesn't matter. That was then, this is now. While your need to cling to a practice you are familiar with may be understandable, it is not desirable. The company you are working for expects you to be effective. The more you hold onto old habits just because you are comfortable with them, the harder you make the transition for yourself and for those trying to train you.

A good learner is receptive, not argumentative and contentious. You want your new boss and co-workers to see you as a person who is eager to learn and do a good job, not as someone who expects those around her to conform to her picture of how the task should be performed based on an old model.

4. Don't compare; don't complain.

Let's say coffee was free in the old place, and here you have to pay for it. There, you had your own filing cabinet, while here you have to share. There, they had express elevators, whereas here they stop at every floor. When adjusting to a new environment, a litany of complaints can issue forth. All these adjustments to make. So much not to your liking. It is sorely tempting to let these little grumblings leak out. Many people who won't do it directly will do it in the form of a joke.

Resist the urge. It does no good at all, and it only creates a bad impression of you. As the saying goes, you only get one chance to create a first impression. Make sure you use it.

> *"History, despite its wrenching pain,*
> *Cannot be unlived, but if faced*
> *With courage, need not be lived again."*
> — *Maya Angelou*

Final Thoughts

To handle the nonstop change that is now a part of life, you will probably have to make a deep and abiding attitude shift, not just brace up for the upcoming change and then settle back into the old mind-set as soon as the waters seem calm again. One woman I talked to told me that when she was thirty-nine facing the "Big Forty," she talked to a lot of friends and did a great deal of journal writing to prepare herself for what she saw as the transition into middle age. The day after her birthday, she sighed with relief that she had made it through the big day without drinking herself into a stupor. Six months later, it occurred to her that she would be turning forty-one. Inexplicably, this came as a shock.

Somewhere in her subconscious, she thought turning forty was the hardest thing she would have to go through and then the whole aging process would stop. It turned out that her forty-first birthday was much harder to bear than the fortieth because that was when it dawned on her that change doesn't stop.

The good news, and if you play chess you know this, is that life is not just a defensive game. The other player — Fate, the World, Corporate America, however you conceive of "the one pulling the strings" — has its own strategy, of course, and you must take that into consideration at all times because it will always affect you. But you must have your strategy developed also, or you are at your opponent's mercy. In other words, you don't win the game by sitting there watching your pawns and your bishops taken down without an idea in your head for taking your opponent's pawns and bishops. Everyone is responsible for his own game plan.

As has been said in previous chapters, when facing the challenges of life, it helps to establish your mission. A mission is not just an immediate goal, even if it is a good one. "I want to have a quarter million dollars in the bank by the time I'm thirty-two." This may satisfy some self-preservation need, but it will not satisfy your soul's need for a higher purpose. As the title of this book suggests, making a living and having a life are inextricably combined. The center of your life, what really drives you, is your greater purpose, and since you spend so much time working, isn't it a good idea to combine the two in some way?

Fortunately, knowing what your true purpose is not only makes you feel more expansive, it actually helps you adjust to and make the most out of change. The long-term goals of a higher purpose keep you on track when plans go awry. They keep you far-sighted so that you don't myopically focus on only the problems in front of you. They motivate you to take proactive steps now that will affect you far into the future. And finally, establishing what your bigger purpose is keeps your mind active and energetic because you are constantly looking at life for opportunities to accomplish your mission.

Since the seventies, the personal growth movement and its influence in the media, as well the proliferation of educational materials, have given us an awareness of how vast human potential really is. Some of us have invested ourselves deeply in this movement. Some have bought the right books and gone to the right talks, but not "digested" and gotten all the nutrition we could out of the knowledge and wisdom we received. Others have studiously shut out anything new in a vain attempt to never rock the boat. And yet, whether we have paid attention or not, these messages of personal growth are all around us. Many people have been pushed into it kicking and screaming, but somehow they have still managed to awaken their own potential.

The constant change of today's world is breaking down old patterns, forcing us to look at our lives with fresh eyes and seek to become the best people we can. Even if the obstacles weren't chosen, overcoming them has taught us that to do so strengthens our character and our resolve. The changes we have met head-on have allowed us to grow.

SUMMARIZED POINTS

1. Sometimes unexpected change is harder to bear than the change you know is coming.

2. There are three stages of change: the end of the old, the interim period, the beginning of the new. Each stage carries its own difficulties.

3. You need to acknowledge and accept grief and all the other negative emotions, if you want to get through them and move on with your life.

4. The in-between stage is often the most difficult. Be patient with yourself.

5. Guard against catastrophic fears.

6. If your identity was propped up by your old job, change offers you the opportunity to find out who you really are without external reinforcement.

7. Genuine beginnings don't take place in an office or in a hallway. They take place in your mind.

CHAPTER NINE

PURPOSE—
THE HEART OF
WISE WORK

*"Everyone has been made for some
particular work, and the desire for that work
has been put into every heart."*
— *Rumi*

It's hard to argue with Rumi, one of the great minds in history and someone who is a model of how to marry the lofty and divine side of life with the practical side. When you mention having a larger purpose to some people, they think they have to leave home and go off on a quest. Or they think they can't afford such a luxury. It takes too much time, too much money, and too much energy. They may be struggling with financial problems or an illness or wayward children, and they don't feel they have the attention to spare. But finding a larger purpose does not take away from life, it gives back to it.

It does, however, take a special kind of energy to discover what your life's purpose is. You have to take some quiet time away from the TV and other distractions and look into yourself deeply. The process might even be a little scary at first. But it is the best gift you will ever give yourself. Fulfilling your unique purpose will be your ultimate satisfaction; it will express the fullness of who you are. It will give meaning to your life and zest to your soul.

The only way you will ever find truly wise work, in fact, is if you discover what your bigger purpose is. Only then can you find your calling. When you know your calling, you have the answer to the most profound question you asked in childhood: "What am I going to do when I grow up?" As adults, we ask what seem to be bigger questions: "Who am I?" or "Why am I here?" What we fail to realize is that all these questions are connected.

> *"Your work is to discover your work,*
> *and then, with all your heart,*
> *to give yourself up to it."*
> — *Buddha*

As we have said many times in this book, work should be about a lot more than collecting a paycheck. Since work time takes up at least a third of our lives, it should count for more than what you can deposit in a bank account. Knowing your purpose will help you be clear about the work you are meant to do.

One other thing people sometimes object to about this kind of soul searching for their own true purpose is that it seems selfish. Interestingly enough, most people find that when they begin doing their real soul work, it also marks the start of a genuine contribution to others. Doing the soul's work usually leaves a lasting legacy to the world.

Tara Lipinski, the Olympic gold medal ice skater, knew what she was meant to do at a very young age. And even as a little girl, she understood that it wouldn't be easy. She had to work hard by getting out on the ice rink at dawn to practice for six hours. By the age of fourteen, she was already dazzlingly good at her "work." It is evident from watching her that a deep satisfaction emanates from within and that she loves what she does. And she has given something back to the world because she brings pleasure to all those who watch her.

Tara was born to skate. We know she has talent, but to achieve what she did, she also had to have an amazing sense of purpose. You don't, however, have to have a glamorous job to feel that a higher principle is guiding your life. No matter who you are or where you work, you can express something that is bigger than you. A shoe salesman with a desire to be in touch with his community and help people might express that by making a personal connection with all his customers and only selling them shoes that are healthy for their feet. A machinist who believes in safety will make strong, flawless parts for the cars that families buy. And like the woman in the following quote, anyone can take enormous pride by acquiring a sense of perfection in her everyday chores.

> *"When I put the plate down, you don't hear a sound. When I pick up a glass, I want it to be just right. When someone says, 'How come you're just a waitress?' I say, 'Don't you think you deserve being served by me?'"*
> — *Studs Terkel*

Tara Lipinski was lucky. She knew what she wanted, and she had parents who encouraged her. So she was able to start out early in life as a wise worker. Unfortunately, many of us were pushed into professions either by parents with extremely conventional ideas or by "guidance" counselors who had a very short list of careers to offer students. And then we stayed in those careers because we liked the money, or we were afraid, or because we just hadn't elevated our thinking yet.

Do not force yourself to fulfill someone else's idea of a career. If you fell into being a doctor but you actually hate the smell of hospitals, how will you ever know that you were meant to be an artist if you just keep methodically showing up for work every day? It is not impossible to be an artist. It only takes courage.

Joseph Campbell said that "if you follow your bliss, you put yourself on a kind of track that has been there all the while, waiting for you, and the life that you ought to be living

201

is the one you are living. When you can see that, you begin to meet people who are in the field of your bliss, and they open the doors to you. I say, follow your bliss and don't be afraid, and doors will open where you didn't know they were going to be. Wherever you are — if you are following your bliss, you are enjoying that refreshment, that life within you, all the time."

Purpose plus Passion Creates Music

Hai

I loved playing the violin from the time I was six. Unlike some children who refuse to practice, I did it daily without being coaxed. When I got to high school, my parents told me playing the violin had been a nice hobby, but now it was time to get serious about my future. Their plan was for me to go to dental school. All I could think was, "But I really don't like looking inside people's mouths." One day in my senior year, my music teacher asked if I would like to take classes with him at the university after I graduated. I wanted to jump at

the chance, and yet I knew my parents would object. I also knew the registration date had passed. He was persistent though. When he asked me again if I was interested I said, "Yes, but ...."
He said, "I only wanted to hear the yes. Let me see what I can do to get you registered." Today, I'm a violin teacher and the concertmaster for a community orchestra. I only go to the dentist's office to get my teeth cleaned.

What Is Purpose and Why Is It a Good Thing?

There are many ways of defining what purpose is. Here are a few:

- The point of existence.

- The reason for which a person, an organization or a group exists.

- One's role in the bigger scheme of things.

As we can see, purpose is big. It is not the same as a goal. A goal is a specific ambition for which you can usually plan definitive steps. A purpose is much grander than that. It is connected to making a contribution to the world, to mankind, to animals, to the environment. If you wish to go after your purpose, however, you need to set goals, and wise work is the avenue you use to set them. This is an example: You have athletic abilities and you want to use them to gain national prominence as a model of how to work hard and lift oneself out of poverty. That's the purpose. You become a football player because it is a sport you love and expresses your innate talent. That's wise work. You plan to make a dazzling touchdown in a big game, which will get you on the cover of *Sports Illustrated,* thereby bringing you into the public eye. That's a goal.

It is quite possible to have goals without a purpose. Lots of people do. Unfortunately, that makes their goal setting short-sighted, and in their case a string of attained goals doesn't amount to very much. Mostly, it just feeds the ego. It is not a satisfying process, and it does not yield a rich experience of life. Fulfilling one's purpose, however, is the ultimate satisfaction.

By getting in touch with your purpose, you invite grace into your life because you recognize that you are tied into the larger world. You actually enter a certain flow where the universe helps you attain your goals. It is amazing how many good things follow just from being in this flow. Since purpose is your reason for being, it draws you to whatever path is right for you.

The Purpose Statement

*"Make your work to be in keeping
with your purpose."*
— Leonardo Da Vinci

It's not so easy to discover what your purpose is in life. Many people have found that it helps to write a purpose statement. Why a statement, and why write it down?

Developing a real, formal statement is different from just letting the first thing that comes into your head be your answer. A statement requires a gestation period. You have to think about it, and then think about it some more. Let it sit for a while. You have to go deeply inside yourself and ask yourself significant questions about who you really are and what you really want. Discovering your sense of purpose is just that — a process of discovery. You do not impose an idea on yourself. Rather, you let yourself be receptive to whatever wants to come out of the depths of you.

People who conceive of their purpose statement often take a long time, weeks or months even. Once they feel that they know what they want to say, they sit down and craft it into words. It is important to write it down on paper. Seeing it in black and white makes it real and concrete. It gives you some perspective. Is that what you really mean, or do you mean something close to that? Another reason for writing the purpose statement is that it makes it a kind of ritual, and that bestows a certain seriousness on the occasion. Rituals have a bonding effect, a way of helping you connect to the fact that you are making a commitment. When two people go through the ritual of getting married, they are making a public commitment to each other. When a person writes a purpose statement, he is making a commitment to himself.

The statement itself has three parts: skills, action, result. You will notice that the wording of the third part — the result — sounds very lofty. It is supposed to be lofty. It must be broad enough that it can encompass all of your goals. Think big. Remember, goals are earthbound but purpose is skybound.

1. Write down three or four of your natural talents or skills.

Limit it to this number because it is more manageable to work with than, say, ten skills. The few that you do pick should be the ones that most attract you, that make you feel passionate when you use them, and that you truly enjoy. In other words, pick your favorites. This will help you see which talents you possess that will probably be best used towards a higher purpose. Then you can see exactly what you have to build on, and you can focus on what you want to use of yourself.

2. Decide what you can actually do with these skills that will benefit yourself and others.

It is important to keep this next part in mind because this is a goal that will work towards a higher purpose than just self-gratification. How, out there in the real world, can you put your unique skills to work.

3. Recognize the end result that you are seeking.

As we said, this will sound lofty, grand, and even celestial — perhaps even out of reach at first. That is all right. You are dipping into a higher part of your consciousness at this point, a part that is capable of embracing life in a very big way. You just might not know it yet.

Here are some examples of how these three parts fit together into one purpose statement.

A. 1. I enjoy humor, acting, and staging performances.

   2. I can use them to entertain and stimulate laughter and fun.

   3. This will bring pleasure and merriment into people's lives.

B. 1. I have good technical, logical and investigative skills.

   2. I will write software programs.

   3. People will be able to work on more user-friendly computers and get more done.

C. 1. I have great mechanical and problem solving abilities.

   2. I will start a garage and repair automobiles.

   3. People will leave my garage in cars that are safe for them and their families.

D. 1. I have always been good at cooking.

   2. I can prepare tasty and exotic meals for people who come to the restaurant.

   3. Food is an important part of life; I can make it a delicious experience.

E. 1. My talents are around sewing, design, and a sense of color in fabric.

2. I can make beautiful and imaginative quilts.

3. People will bring real, homespun beauty into their homes.

F. 1. My best areas are communication, compassion, creativity and enthusiasm.

2. I want to impact and empower people through the written and spoken word.

3. When they are empowered they will be able to have lives filled with peace, love, and joy. (the author's own purpose statement)

Some people, like Hai who loves to play the violin and Tara who loves to skate, never had to struggle to discover what their purpose was. They could have written their purpose statement over a cup of coffee. For others, it is far more difficult. One easy practice to stimulate your mind is to write down all your natural talents and skills, or the things you enjoy, or the kinds of activities that have meaning for you. See if you can discern a pattern for yourself, something that emerges from the clutter that has a sense of direction to it. Two other things you can do are use your intuition and cast your mind back over your personal history and look for signs.

Let Intuition Be Your Guide

Many of us need to do some inner detective work to find something we may have lost touch with — our intuition. Intuition is the messenger that will make your true purpose clear to you.

There is a climactic moment during a fight in one of the *Star Wars* movies, when Ben Kenobi says to Luke Skywalker, "Turn off your computer, turn off your machine, and do it yourself. Follow your feelings, trust your feelings." This science fiction sage is talking about gut feelings. Another way to say it is intuition or inner knowing. You won't find intuition on an amusement park ride or in a classroom or at the gym. As Ben would say, you can only find the source within you. Deep inside lie all the answers that will enlighten your mind and engage your imagination, leading you to purposeful, wise work.

Janelle

I had an MBA from an Ivy League college and a great career track record. Yet after twenty years of continuous upward movement in the corporate world, I got laid off. I figured I ought to take advantage of my severance package which, in part, consisted of high-level outplacement services. I went to the orientation program, but after about a half hour I almost fainted. That's how great my resistance was to being there. My body was trying to tell me something, but I kept writing my feelings off to anger and resentment about losing my job. In reality, I was getting a bold signal — that I would rather pass out than stay in this profession. Finally, I realized I wasn't listening to the speaker at all, and I left.

I had always ignored my intuition. There had been other cues earlier in my career that I was in the wrong place, but I just used to put on my Energizer Bunny suit and keep going. A battery of tests for personality and career assessment had already warned me I was going in a direction that was unsuitable for me personally. "We don't know what you should be doing," the testers said, "but we know you shouldn't be doing what you're doing now." During that orientation program, it took every bone in my body protesting to get me to finally listen to the messages the universe was giving me.

We all have this inner capacity called intuition. It's there just to help us. We actually use it all the time without realizing it. Have you ever driven through a strange neighborhood and just known which way to turn? Or sensed that someone was upset with you even though he had a smile plastered on his face? These are the little ways intuition shows up in our lives. What we need to do is learn to pay attention to it about the big things so that we stay on track in our lives. If you want to know what your bigger purpose is in life and what wise work is for you, let your inner knowing act as a guidance counselor.

Michael

During the recession, my twenty-five year career came to an end. Just before I left, the company president invited me out for dinner. He said something very strange to me. "You know what I'm going to remember about you? I'll remember what you eat." Not the major IMS system I had spent three years developing, not the ten extra hours I put in every week — what I eat! Something seemed wrong here if, after everything I had contributed, this was how I was going to be remembered.

In the period immediately following the loss of my job, I went through so much stress that I developed asthma. Deciding that it was probably a psychological reaction to being out of work, I consulted a therapist. She sent me to an acupuncturist for the asthma. Years before, I had had an avid interest in acupuncture, but it never seemed like a real career choice, so I had put it out of my mind. I really enjoyed the sessions with the acupuncturist (who later became my Tai Chi teacher). As I began to feel better physically, I started to get in touch with my deeper feelings, and it made me wonder if this wasn't something I might like to do for a living myself. But my path is a path of doubt. What I

209

*had to find out was that just because you have
doubts, it doesn't mean you're making the wrong
choice. I know people who are always clear about
what they're doing. I'm not one of them. I realized
that I had never paid attention to the messages I
was getting before because I thought they should
be crystal clear. I now know that intuition is very
subtle.*

I'm sure you've heard the expression, "There are no coincidences." Isn't it interesting that events in Michael's life kept leading him in the right direction, that something in him kept the dream alive? In the end though, as with Janelle, events had to take a dramatic turn before he would pay attention to the *dream cues*. Not only is Michael on the road to a successful career in the health field now, but he finally has a meaningful life.

To Find More Clues, Search Your Own Past

> *"And to love life through labour is to be
> intimate with life's inmost secret."*
> — *Kahlil Gibran*

Steven Spielberg spent much of his childhood watching movies and then went on to become the most successful director of all time. Kenny G spent hours playing the saxophone when he was a boy and went on to become a gold-record-winning musician. While I may be less famous than those two, I can look back on my life and see the auspicious signs of what I was to become. The work I do now directly mirrors my lifelong values and issues.

To help you on the path of discovery, ask yourself these questions:

- What are some of the patterns that have run through my life?

- What type of people have I always enjoyed being around?

- What things always gave me pleasure?

- What activities did I hate?

- What motivated me to overcome challenges?

- What have I done with my spare time?

- What did I dream about being when I was young?

- What kinds of books did I take out of the library?

- What activities were so engrossing they made the day fly by?

- What kinds of activities was I drawn to over and over?

The answers are there if you look for them, hidden in the past. For some people, the answers are written all over their personal history. I know of a nurse who loves her work. Every day, she feels like she is doing something truly worthwhile. When she was a little girl, she always needed to bring her mother a cup of hot tea when she had a cold. Even among her friends, she was known as a caretaker. It was natural for her to grow up and put her nurturing personality to work taking care of the sick. For other people, the answers come at them little more indirectly. These people become what they do to make up for the past. One man I spoke to became a therapist to learn how to listen to people. When he was a boy, he was ignored, and he realized more than his peers did how important it was for all people to have somebody listen to them.

As is shown by the questions above, there are a number of different ways to approach this kind of detective work. You can look at your wishes and dreams, at your best qualities, at what you most enjoyed doing on a summer day, or at your skills. Quite often, when you uncover hidden skills or desires, you find that they can lead you in a number of directions. For instance, the desire to be an artist may show up in a job teaching art to children or a career as an art therapist. Our course in life is more limited by a lack of imagination than by anything else. How many people who think they cannot make a living being an artist think they have to give up and work at the local fast food place? It doesn't occur to them that they can channel their deepest desire into a relevant career that uses what is inside of them in other ways.

To Make Your Higher Purpose a Reality — Visualize It

A vision is a mental image of what your true path will look like when you start to live it. You see it through the power of your imagination. It is an excellent tool for drawing your hopes and dreams towards you.

A vision is a picture that you create in your mind. The source for what the picture looks like is your own desires. What do you want your future to be? Play it out in your head like a story over and over again. In the story, what actions do you take to get what you want?

Let the vision expand and merge with your wish list. This means you really have to get in touch with what you desire. The sky is the limit. Let your mind run free. Only then can you be sure that what your soul wants to reach for is really being expressed. When letting your vision unfold, don't try to be too practical or "realistic." Above all, keep all money and time constraints out of the picture. If you notice the little practical, sensible part of yourself wagging its finger and interfering, stepping in with all those annoying limits, tell it to go away. This is a time for you to be generous with yourself and return to the brilliant and lustrous imagination of your childhood.

> *"You will not be asked why you were not perfect or successful or rich. You will be asked why you were not you."*
> — *Rabbi Zusya*

For your vision to be all-encompassing and rich in detail, incorporate the following ideas:

- the values you hold dear
- the inherent talents and skills you need to fulfill your goals
- your personal strengths that will help you succeed
- the type of people you like to be around
- the kind of service it enriches you to perform
- what gives you joy and pleasure.

In sports, they have known for a long time that if you can't see yourself doing it, you can't do it. Visualizing is just that important. Trainers have skiers play a ski jump over and over in their mind before they actually make the jump. The athletes try to imagine every single detail as it will be, and as they would will it to be, for the perfect jump. Trainers and athletes both know from experience the power that the mind and imagination play in performance. So once you know what your path is, visualize it as clearly as if it were a movie being shown on a screen right in front of you. In this movie, you play four roles: you are the script writer, the producer, the director, and the main actor.

Form a Purpose Group

In this society of the individualist mentality, where the archetype is a picture of a lone cowboy on a horse setting out toward the horizon, we fail to recognize how much we, as human beings, genuinely need support. And we especially need that support when going after a higher purpose. After all, it's not as easy as playing a game of Monopoly. There are all kinds of difficulties that need to be faced. Often, when people see what their true purpose is in life, the first things they encounter are psychological blocks to achieving it: inertia, fear, low self-esteem, "habit" thinking that keeps them stuck in their old conventional ideas. Whenever we want to make a big change, that is the time we need to actively seek support.

A support group is the ideal forum for keeping your sense of purpose high and for building energy for its evolution. A group of people who are as interested as you are in discovering their higher purpose and living it will act as a mainstay for you.

People will be people, and when they get together in a group to talk about something serious, there will always be the tendency to stray off the subject, to tell stories and jokes, or discuss the latest scandal in the news. That is why it is important to follow an established agenda for your meetings. The very structure helps keep everyone on track. What is also true about groups is that they are made up of all kinds of people, some shy and some talkative. An established agenda will provide a certain amount of time for everyone to speak, particularly those who wouldn't ordinarily want any attention. To make sure that there is enough time to spread out evenly, keep the number of people in the group small — six to ten at the most.

The following is a sample agenda that I have used successfully:

7:00–7:30 PM Declaration of purpose statement and check-in.

Go around the circle and let each person state her purpose. It doesn't matter if the statement is worded exactly the same from one week to the next or if it is the most perfect, final statement. We are all in a state of flux, and as people get clearer, the wording of their purpose statements gets clearer and clearer. This is also the period during which each person reports, briefly, on what new accomplishment or idea she had that week that contributed to the fulfillment of her purpose.

7:30–8:30 PM Work-related conversation.

Once again, go around the circle in an established order. Let everyone discuss any problems she has had in the course of the past week that relate to either her work or her purpose. Group members may need advice or backing for dealing with a difficult boss, or for seeking out creative new ways to develop opportunities for themselves that use their innate talents. People who are currently out of work will need encouragement for their job search. Members often put the problem out there and then request some brainstorming for new ideas and for feedback, or for an approach they haven't thought of themselves. The group can tell the person what skills they could be using but aren't. It is not uncommon for others to see more in you than you see in yourself. The greatest support of all comes when they point out your blind spots to you. The perspective of others can help you make your life bigger by increasing your sense of who you are.

8:30–9:00 PM Commitment for the following week.

Talk is cheap. If you leave the meeting without discussing what you are going to do with all your newfound ideas, you have not done your job. In this step, each person presents a plan of action for the week coming up. It may be a big plan or a small plan. The important thing is that it address the problem and not side-step it. There is a built-in incentive to being practical and sensible in conceptualizing this plan — members know they will be asked to report on how well they carried it out at the subsequent meeting. Finish with words of appreciation and encouragement all around, and then confirm the next week's time and location.

> *"Nothing less than finding what you were meant to be and do will give you the motivation and the capability that today's work world demands. Identifying your life work is no longer an escapist fantasy. It is a condition of being successful."*
> —William Bridges

Final Thoughts

You have talents you know about and talents you don't. They are both crying to be let out of you and to be used. You also have skills and abilities. All of this makes up your potential, and inherent within potential is the need that it be actualized. Can you feel what your potential really is, or does low self-esteem and limited vision keep you from seeing it?

> *"Where your talents and the needs of the world cross, there lies your vocation."*
> —Aristotle

Your talents are your innate gifts. You are born with them. All they ask is that you discover them, develop them, and employ them well. As you use wise work in the service of a greater purpose to draw out those gifts, you will find that a profound new excitement and pleasure will fill your days because you are doing what expresses you in your own unique way. And because purpose is naturally connected to the greater whole, you will be giving something back to the community, whether that community is your own neighborhood or the entire planet.

Oliver Wendell Holmes said: "Don't die with the music still inside of you." That is the poetic way of telling you not to make the mistake of wasting your life by not fulfilling your potential.

SUMMARIZED POINTS

1. The way to find wise work is to discover your purpose.

2. Do not force yourself to fulfill someone else's idea of a career.

3. Follow your bliss, and you put yourself on a kind of wise track to success that has been there all the while waiting for you.

4. A purpose is not the same as a goal; it is something larger.

5. By getting in touch with your purpose, you invite grace into your life because you feel yourself tied into the larger world.

6. Discovering your sense of purpose is just that — a process of discovery.

7. Writing a purpose statement helps form your thinking and gives you the perspective of seeing it in black and white.

8. Let intuition make your true purpose clear to you.

9. Just because you have doubts, it doesn't mean you're making the wrong choice.

10. Form a purpose group with like-minded people so that you can support each other in setting goals that are in alignment with your bigger sense of purpose.

CHAPTER TEN

BALANCE — WORKING AND HAVING A LIFE

*"Work is the skillful expression of our total
being, our means to create harmony and
balance within ourselves and in the world."*
— *Tarthang Tulku*

In Eastern philosophy they know that nothing exists without its opposite. How would you know to call something beautiful if you had never seen anything that was ugly? What is up without down, or dark without light? We always think we prefer one side of the opposite over the other, like a hot fudge sundae instead of canned peas.

Therese

When I was a little girl, my best friend Vicki and I used to ask each other, "If you were stranded on a desert island and you could have only one food, what would it be?" I don't know why we thought this was such a burning question, but we tried really hard to answer it. I would think of my favorite foods, the ones my mother would hardly ever let me have, like strawberries dipped in the sugar bowl. For a moment it seemed like heaven to eat my one favorite thing all the time. But then I thought about how it would be the third day and the fourth day on the island. Strawberries with sugar. Then I thought about a week later, waking up in the morning to — strawberries again.

Too much of any one thing creates imbalance, and balance is one of life's great necessities. The biggest misconception most people have about opposites is that work is the opposite of play. The fact that we believe these two are diametrically opposed is built into how we talk. TGIF is a phrase we have all grown up with — "Thank God It's Friday." We don't say "Thank God It's Monday" because that is the start of the dreaded work week. Work is characterized by labor and drudgery, and play is characterized by recreation and amusement. While there are real differences between your work and what we call play, they do not have to be at odds with each other. On the contrary, they can balance each other.

Balance is not something you do, it is a state of being. It produces an inner sense of joy, equanimity, and harmony. Balance feels from the inside, but acts from the outside. When we are in this state, it becomes the ground from which everything else proceeds. Becoming balanced in our work is the route for putting our good will and our plans into action. It becomes our opportunity to bring what is inside us to the outside, to make a gift of our personal resources to the world.

Work Has Its Own Special Niche

There may be many ways in which a person's life can feel out of balance:

- Too much sitting around and not enough exercise.

- Taking care of the kids all day and never being able to go out and have lunch with the girls.

- Spending free time mowing the lawn instead of pursuing a hobby.

- Too much time with people and not enough time alone.

- Too much emphasis on what you should do and not enough on what you prefer to do.

Almost everyone can relate to these points, even if they aren't currently a problem. We are always trying to create balance between two things, both of which are pulling on us in seemingly different directions. Balance in general, then, is a constant issue. But the type of job we have poses a special balance problem. Work is more of a loaded issue, usually, than exercise or hobbies or social matters. You can add points of your own to the following list, but this is an inventory of twelve significant ways in which work is perceived as different from every other area of our lives:

1. Virtually all of us are under some direct authority at work, whereas at home and with friends, we are on a more equal footing.

2. Our company seems to have tremendous power over us because without a paycheck, we believe we cannot eat or put a roof over our heads. In other words, your friends don't hand over money to you every other Friday so you can pay your mortgage, but your company does.

3. Most people's experience, especially when they aren't particularly enamored of their jobs, is that they have to perform tasks that are not conducive to their temperament.

4. We have to operate on someone else's time frame. Most of us would not set our alarm clocks to get up at six o'clock in the morning if we didn't have to punch in at the office by eight.

5. We give up some basic freedoms, ones we take for granted at home but do not enjoy at work. We cannot eat lunch when we are hungry; for example, we have to eat when our boss tells us it is our lunch hour.

6. These days, the forty-hour week seems to be a thing of the past. We have to stay somewhere we don't want to be in the first place, for a longer period of time than we are supposed to.

7. We have to be in an environment we don't want to be in because that is where the work is. I know of people who work in huge skyscrapers, and they desperately wish they could be outside on a beautiful day. They don't mind working. They just want to be out in the sunshine instead of in an unnatural, air-conditioned office.

8. After a few years of working, most of us have figured out that because we are the ones who perform the functions of our job all day, we know the intricacies of it better than anyone. Yet our boss can decide that something should be done a certain way when we know instinctively that he is wrong. At work, someone can *make* you perform inefficiently.

9. The skills we are really good at are not the ones that get used. So we are performing all day long using skills that do not come naturally, and the ones that do come naturally lie fallow.

10. To get to our jobs, we have to commute at exactly the same times as everyone else. Not everybody falls into this category, of course, but most Americans do. When we do other things in our lives that involve traveling some distance, like running errands or taking the car in for a tune-up, we make sure we do it when there is the least amount of traffic. For work, we don't have that luxury, and end up sitting in rush hour traffic two hours a day.

11. We don't get to choose the people we spend eight to ten hours a day with. We choose our mates. We choose our friends. We do not choose our co-workers.

12. Many people need to repress their personality when they get to work because it doesn't fit in with that particular environment. Someone may have a very talkative and social type of personality that is frowned upon in her job as a

medical clerk. She is expected to be formally polite to people who enter the office and not tell them a funny story about what happened to her over the weekend.

Wise Work Is Different

When we talk about finding a good balance, we are not saying that all twelve of the above problems, or any of the others that may appear on your own list, will disappear. We are not saying that you have to search the globe for a job where everything is precisely to your liking. What we are saying is that when you are engaged in wise work, what you do all day expresses who you are, and that allows you to stay in a natural state of balance. Because what you are doing is inherently fulfilling, you experience equanimity no matter what is going on around you. I know of many people who happily get in their cars and enter rush hour traffic because they are heading towards a destination where they genuinely want to be. If they could avoid the stop-and-go of traffic, of course they would, but because they are in a state of joy and satisfaction, the picky little things they have to go through in the course of a day are overshadowed.

> *"I never did a day's work in my life.*
> *It was all fun."*
> — *Thomas Edison*

Wise work feels a lot like play. You are engaged and interested, you care very much about the outcome, and it actually gives you pleasure to be doing it. Thomas Jefferson wrote that "It is neither wealth nor splendor, but tranquillity and occupation, which give happiness." When we can see work as more than just a way to make a living, when we see it as a way to use ourselves and actualize our potential, then it can enrich our experience and make us even happier than a good tennis match or a night at the movies or a day at the races.

Who ever said work couldn't be fun? Like the Seven Dwarfs, we can whistle while we work if it is the work we were always meant to be doing.

Angelica

When I was twenty-six, something inside me said, "If it's fun, it can't be work." If I wasn't suffering, I couldn't take myself seriously and thought I was behaving like a child. When I looked through the want ads, I always ended up selecting interviews for jobs I had no disposition for, like a secretary or an accountant. One day I got a card from my mother that read, "Follow your dreams. So as you dream, you shall become." I don't know who wrote it, but it was as if those words spoke directly to me. I took them as permission to follow my dream and give up my relentless pursuit of what I thought an adult should be doing. For the past twenty years I have been working on luxury ships as a cruise director. I've been able to meet a lot of interesting people and travel all over the world. That was my dream. That's what I've become.

Wise work creates balance because it allows us to transform all of our true potential into action that actually makes a difference in the world. You can't often say that about play. Going to an amusement park for the day may do a lot for you, but it doesn't contribute much to anyone else's life. Wise work, on the other hand, gives you a sense of accomplishment in addition to the joy of engaging in activities that use your skills. Being productive in a way that is genuinely useful to others is a natural drive, and only work can truly satisfy that drive.

Think of a river that is flowing unimpeded downhill. When we have balance in our work, that is our natural state. There is no discord between who we are at work and who we are at home. At my workshops, I have people take behavioral profiles to see what their natural predilections are. They often fill out the profile according to their "work personality," not their "home personality." In other words, they describe themselves as they are when they are fulfilling their company's criteria, not as they are in their natural state. When I ask them, "Is that how you are at home?" all too often the answer is no. I always think it is a shame that so many people lead work lives that force them to abandon who they really are.

It's As Personal As Fingerprints

Whatever meaning you attach to the words *work* and *play*, the secret to balance is how they offset and complement each other. How do we acquire the ability to blend work and play? We just go out and do it. Where do we get the freedom so that we can design our lives to be what we want them to be? We just do it. If you are waiting for permission from some voice in the clouds, or even one in your head, you may end up waiting a long time. Just do it.

There is no one set of instructions for everyone because each of us is so unique. Just as no one else has our fingerprint, no one else has our temperament, our values, attitudes, style, preferences, interests, background, or skills. All of these combine in a singular way to form who we are, and who we are dictates what balance will work just for us. There is an old saying, "I march to a different drummer." The truth is that everybody marches to a different drummer, to their own unique tune, and to find the rhythm that is right for you, you need to use your personal tuning fork.

We all have different attitudes, which are reflected in the way we think. Some people think linearly, logically, and rationally, while others think intuitively, creatively, or poetically. What kind of thinker we are heavily sways how we balance our time. A linear thinker may conceive of a fun time as going to hear an engineer talk about earthquake proofing. A creative thinker would rather hear chamber music.

We all have different styles. Our style is reflected in our behavior. Some people are very active, while others are laid back. Some like to get right to work in the morning, while others would rather do the *New York Times* crossword puzzle first. For a person who is movement-oriented, a day of lying on the beach would be torture. Yet for the one who loves the space to just contemplate life, he is willing to wait all year for that week when he can just sit and watch the waves rhythmically wash in to shore. Your personal style will also influence the type of work you choose. If you are a highly structured individual, you will be attracted to a hierarchical environment where your role is neatly defined. If you hang together a little looser, you will prefer working for yourself and setting your own hours.

We all have different values. Our values influence the type of choices we make. They are our guiding principles, and they form our standards. They also sway how we balance our lives. Many people would feel their lives were out of balance if they were not doing service-oriented work, while others would feel the same if they were not doing creative work. Since balance is a state of mind, whether or not we live in accord with our values dictates whether we live in harmony with ourselves. When we go against our values, the internal struggle robs us of all peace of mind.

Do What Works For You

Justin

For me, work is a piece of a whole that includes living in an area I like, raising a family, and doing the work I excel at. Years ago, I decided that my work was as integral a part of my life as anything else was and that I would incorporate it into the entire mosaic. I have had a job with the same large service organization for twenty-two years now, and I have managed to get myself transferred to positions in the cities I have wanted to live in. My family is happy, and so am I.

Justin has found the secret to balance. He has done it his way. Instead of looking at pie charts, or demographics, or others people's ideas, he has sought out his own equilibrium. He made conscious choices to live and work where he wanted. You, too, need to seek a work and lifestyle that are balanced in a way that suits you. And only you can design it.

One thing to consider that a lot of people overlook is the fact that not only are you different from other people, you are different from yourself as you were at various other points in your life. When we are young, we are usually more adventurous, more preoccupied with having fun, pursuing romantic interests, and trying new things. We may also be more ambitious, eager to burn up the world. That will dictate what type of job will suit our temperament. When we enter our fifties, however, and we have already done a lot of moving and shaking, we often want to settle in one place and enjoy more time off. We look for stability and security instead. Again, that will dictate the best job for us. Training Navy S.E.A.L.S. in the North Atlantic will not be a good choice for someone whose greatest pleasure in the day is filling the hummingbird feeder.

On the other hand, sometimes people want to work more hours in a day when they get older because it isn't until later in life that they find the work they love.

Anne

When I was younger, I was an engineering designer. I used to dread getting up to catch the bus out to the government lab I worked at. Although I had a degree, I was never any good at my job, and I had to bluff my way through the day. It's very depressing when you're stuck in a career you know you'll never be any good at. One Sunday, I went rollerblading in the park. I took a bad fall, and hurt my back. After that, I could no longer lean over a drafting board all day. For a year, I had to rest up while I waited for my back to get better, and during that time, I started doing something I had always wanted to do — write. In the course of writing and rewriting my first book, I finally figured out that what I was really and truly good at was editing. My brain was built to edit. Now, I have a full practice doing what I do best. I have never wanted to get to work in the morning the way I do now. It took me thirty years, but I finally figured out what I was meant to be in life.

This happens a lot. It is not uncommon for people to pick the wrong careers at first. They are young. They don't know much about the world, and they don't know much about themselves. It is ridiculous to ask a sixteen-year-old in the eleventh grade to decide what he wants to do with the rest of his life — he barely knows what he wants to do over the weekend. Also, he hasn't had enough experience to make an informed choice. Once Anne found a job that let her develop her innate talents, even though she was fifty, she suddenly became as ambitious as most twenty-year-olds are. For her at age twenty, a good life had meant working as few hours a day as possible. Now she gets bored if she doesn't work every day. It often isn't until you are older that you discover what it is that will fully engage your interests, skills, and talents in a perfectly blended way. When this does happen, though, you fall in love with your work.

As we mature, we also add new experiences to our lives and adopt a vast and varied range of ideas. In gaining a wider perspective, people often have a change of values, which causes them to reapportion how they use their time and energy. Men who missed out on their own children's youth because they were busy climbing the corporate ladder, for example, will take an active interest in the lives of their grandchildren. Our interests change. Did you know that the median age of gardeners in this country is fifty-one? This means that very few eighteen-year-olds are interested in growing their own vegetables, but the same person who couldn't tell the difference between soil amendments and sand at eighteen finds, at fifty-five, that nothing gives her greater pleasure than picking salad ingredients from her own garden.

Don't get stuck in pursuing the same interests all your life just because you've never stopped to question whether your tastes have changed. What are you really interested in now? Is it bike riding, listening to jazz, sailing, learning new languages, going to the theater, scuba diving, traveling, or reading? Is it working harder or working less? A list of all the different interests that are possible could fill its own book. Yet out of all of them, virtually no two people would make the same choices. And of the entire list, we would pick only a few activities with which to fill our time.

If Joe Smith's main interest is his job, for example, he will enjoy working fifty hours a week. On the weekend, he will check out old cars, take his kids to the beach, and go see a play or a movie with his wife and friends. These are among the five or six favorite things he likes to do with his time, and they make him feel complete. If any one of them were missing for any period of time, he would be thrown off balance. But if skydiving, something he has never wanted to do in his life, *were* missing (unlike his neighbor who lives to skydive on weekends), it wouldn't bother him a bit. To each his own. I want to point out here that just because Joe loves his work, it does not mean he has a driven personality, that he is compelled to stay at the office until he drops, and to neglect his family. Those people are the working challenged. Joe is just a guy whose work genuinely engages him — and he has a life, too.

For many people, neither work nor leisure activities alone satisfy all their needs, but together, they balance each other. For instance, I know a woman who is very good at her job as a reference librarian, helping university professors find the material they need to write their papers. However, she also has an athletic streak in her, so at night after work, she jogs five miles. By the time she gets home she has exercised her brain and her body and is in a state of perfect equilibrium within herself. Work doesn't have to provide for every single requirement, nor do our off-hour activities. To have balance, we need to design a work and home life that incorporates all facets of our personality.

If, in reading this chapter, it occurs to you that you have no idea what lifestyle really works for you, then you need to go back and do the exercises in this book that are designed to help you find out what it is. You may also need to work with the core beliefs that keep you from believing you deserve to have a life you love, or that convince you you cannot go out and win it for yourself.

Once you can honestly and clearly see what you want your work and life to be like, the whole balance of work and play changes. With your fantastic new job, you may find that work expresses who you are, and you don't have to play so hard on weekends to express yourself. Now that writing cutting-edge computer programs turns you on from Monday through Friday, waterskiing isn't quite as enchanting as it used to be. Why? Because waterskiing doesn't utilize all your mental and creative skills. It is a nice sideline, it's fun, but it does not engage your rich, innate, personal talents the way your work does.

Work As a Facilitator for Life Balance

Working people often envy the idle rich, but they shouldn't. They only do it because they have not come to appreciate what working has done for their lives and their character. The external imperative of having to make a living has forced them beyond the narrowness of how they used to see themselves and their capabilities. If external forces had not made them go out there and prove themselves, they might have sat on a couch all day and watched life go by. Not only have they had to function in ways and according to standards outside their normal realm of experience, but they have had to get along with a diverse group of people, expanding their awareness of what a human being is and how we are all meant to live with each other.

What does all this have to do with balance? If you are not using all the parts of yourself, you are not in balance. It's just that simple. Work forces you to use more parts of yourself than you ever would for anything else, and even if you haven't seen it happening, it has brought balance into your life. Wise work allows us the even greater balance of being true to ourselves and being out in the world at the same time. For to be authentically oneself *and* in the world is the epitome of the balanced life.

In Chapter One, I defined wise work as using the whole of yourself. When you connect with your innate skills, talents, and creativity, you know that you are doing what you were born to do. You are actualizing your potential, and everything you produce is a natural expression of who you are.

Integration: A Balanced Life

Once you are involved in wise work, your life takes on a sense of purpose. By integrating work with all the other aspects of who you are, you become fulfilled in a way you never could have envisioned. Your life takes on the rich texture of a tapestry and the rhythm of a poem. I say that it is when you have gone from *making a living* to *having a life*.

SUMMARIZED POINTS

1. Balance is not something you do, it is a state of being.

2. For many people, neither work nor leisure activities alone satisfy all their needs, but together they balance each other.

3. When you are engaged in wise work, what you do all day expresses who you are, and that allows you to stay in a natural state of balance.

4. Because what you are doing is inherently fulfilling, you experience equanimity no matter what is going on around you.

5. There is no one set of instructions for everyone because each of us is unique.

6. Our values influence the type of choices we make. They also sway how we balance our lives.

7. As people mature, they add new experiences and ideas to their lives. In gaining a wider perspective, people often go through a change of values causing them to reprioritize what they do with their time.

8. If you are not using all the parts of yourself, you are not in balance.

THE WISDOM OF LIFE'S LESSONS

The people I interviewed for this book learned a number of important lessons, which they were able to integrate into their lives. Since we can also learn from other people's experiences, let them be a gift to you on your personal journey to a happier, peaceful, and more fulfilled work life.

Know Thyself

- Self-examination is a healthy habit to get into. When life goes awry, ask yourself why it happened, what role you played, and what you can learn from it.

- To thine own self be true.

- It is not what you do, but who you are that counts.

- Let intuition be your guide.

- When you don't have a clear picture of yourself and your place in the scheme of things, you feel lost and vulnerable. Life is harder, more of a struggle.

- I have integrity when what I hold in my heart, in my thoughts, in my words, and in my actions are all aligned.

Change

- Weathering change with grace contributes to your own growth and spiritual evolution.

- Real change doesn't have to occur with one huge effort. It can happen through the accumulation of small efforts every single day.

- Change your attitude and you change your life.

- A job that is too comfortable is not a good thing. It doesn't challenge you to grow, personally or professionally.

- The journey of a thousand miles begins with the first step. If you want things to change, you have to take that step.

- It is much easier to adjust your lifestyle than you would imagine.

- There is no such thing as security.

- Embrace and promote change. It's going to happen anyway.

- Learn to grieve for your losses and let go.

- Pick yourself up, dust yourself off, and carry on.

Rewards

- When you are happy with what you do, energy is bountiful.

- With meaningful work, you know you are making a difference.

- If you can imagine it and take action toward it, you can make anything happen.

- Taking control over your life makes you feel more vital, and it makes you a force to be reckoned with.

- The more you do, the more you are affirmed.

Take Risks

- Try something new every day. A little bit of risk keeps life exciting.

- No matter what happens or how bad it is, it can be used as a learning experience.

- It's as important to find out where not to work as it is where you should be working.

- Learn new lessons every chance you get.

- Strengthen your weaknesses, but focus on improving your strengths.

- Open the door to new possibilities. If they're interesting, play with them a while.

- Be courageous — if you really want to do something, give it a try.

- The hardest lesson is learning how to just allow the process to take place.

- Make sure the risks you take are not reckless, but calculated.

- As doubt arises, just keep going. The more you forge ahead, the more the doubt will subside.

Don't Stay with the Negatives

- Train yourself to think more positively.

- You don't get points for suffering. If you're unhappy where you work, leave for someplace better.

- Anything is possible, so never give up.

- It's worse to be trapped in a job you hate than to leap into the unknown and look for a new one.

- Don't make yourself work at a job you are not temperamentally suited for.

- Don't take a job that doesn't feel right just because it comes with a good paycheck.

- Money is a good servant. Don't let it be the boss.

- Love people and use money. Don't love money and use people.

- Fear is stifling to the spirit.

- Don't take failure personally. Every apparent failure is just another step toward success.

- Don't let negative people bring you down and influence how you think.

How to Do It

- Find your own particular joy and passion, and make that your work.

- Use a career-focused workbook to help you dwell on your strengths.

- Attend meetings for unemployed professionals to learn how to get back into the work world, and find out what you would like to do next.

- Become a good networker.

- Create or find a support group with people who are going through the same changes you are.

- Timing is everything. You have to be tuned in to recognize when it's time to take the plunge.

- Be honest, have integrity, work hard, do a good job, and take care of yourself.

- Have compassion for others.

- Love yourself.

- Speak up for yourself.

- Stick by your principles.

- Don't work for an organization that is not aligned with your personal values.

- Take responsibility for the choices you make.

As you wander on to work, friends,
Whatever be your path,
Keep your eye upon your lessons,
Not upon life's wrath.
For as you grow into who you are,
Wisdom grows in you as well,
As the lessons take on meaning,
Your work and life will jell.
With life's many joys and pleasures
That were in you all the time,
Your bounty of special treasures
Will keep your life sublime.

— The Author
(in one of her poetic moments)

Bibliography

American Institute of Stress, Research Materials, Yonkers, NY

Bolles, Richard, *What Color Is Your Parachute?*, Ten Speed Press, Berkeley, 1998

Bridges, William, *Creating You & Company*, Addison-Wesley, Reading, MA, 1997

Bridges, William, *Job Shift*, Addison-Wesley, Reading, MA, 1994

Bridges, William, *Managing Transitions*, Addison-Wesley, Reading, MA, 1991

Campbell, Joseph, *The Power of Myth*, Doubleday, New York, 1988

CQ Researcher, published by Congressional Quarterly, Inc., 1995

Davidson, Jeff, *Idiot's Guide to Managing Stress*, Alpha Books, New York, 1997

Davidson, Jeff, *Breathing Space*, MasterMedia Limited, New York, 1991

Finley, Guy, *The Secrets of Letting Go*, Llewellyn Publications, St. Paul, MN, 1996

Fritz, Robert, *The Path of Least Resistance*, Ballantine Books, New York, 1989

Garfield, Charles, *Peak Performers*, Avon, New York, 1986

Gibran, Kahlil, *The Prophet*, Alfred A. Knopf, New York, 1984

Guterman, Mark, *Common Sense for Uncommon Times*, Consulting Psychologists Press, Inc., Palo Alto, CA, 1994

Harris, Louis and Associates, Inc., *The American Workforce Survey of Full-Time Workers*, Conducted for Interim Services, Inc., New York, 1997

Hegarty, Christopher, *How to Manage Your Boss*, Ballantine, New York, 1990

Kofodimos, Joan, *Balancing Act*, Jossey-Bass, Inc., San Francisco, 1993

Leider, Richard J., *The Power of Purpose*, Berrett-Koehler Publishers, Inc., San Francisco, 1997

Naisbitt, John and Patricia Aburdene, *Megatrends 2000*, William Morrow and Company, Inc., New York, 1990

Nelson, Portia, *There's a Hole in My Sidewalk*, Beyond Words Publishing Inc., 1980

Patent, Arnold, *You Can Have It All*, Beyond Words Publishing, Inc., Hillsboro, Oregon, 1995

Schmidt, Warren Ph.D., *The Winds of Change* (Video), Barr Films

Scott, Cynthia D. and Dennis T. Jaffe, *Take This Job and Love It*, Crisp Publications, Menlo Park, CA, 1997

Shenk, David, *Data Smog*, HarperEdge, San Francisco, 1997

Terkel, Studs, *Working*, Pantheon, New York, 1974

Tulku, Tarthang, *Skillful Means*, Dharma Publishing, Berkeley, 1991

Additional Suggested Readings

Intuition

Emery, Marcia, Ph.D., *Intuition Workbook, An Expert's Guide to Unlocking the Wisdom of Your Subconscious Mind*, Prentice Hall, Englewood Cliffs, NJ, 1994

Peirce, Penney, *The Intuitive Way: A Guide to Living from Inner Wisdom*, Beyond Words Publishing, Inc., Hillsboro, Oregon, 1997

Rosanoff, Nancy, *Intuition Workout: A Practical Guide to Discovering and Developing Your Inner Knowing*, Aslan Publishing, Santa Rosa, CA, 1991

Problem Solving

Dawson, Roger, *The Confident Decision Maker*, Nightingale-Conant, Chicago, 1993

Gelatt, Ed.D., H.B., *Creative Decision Making: Using Positive Uncertainty*, Crisp Publications, Inc., Los Altos, California, 1991

Michalko, Michael, *Tinker Toys*, Ten Speed Press, Berkeley, 1991

Plunkett, Lorne C. and Guy A. Hale, *The Proactive Manager: The Complete Book of Problem Solving and Decision Making*, John Wiley & Sons Inc., New York, 1982

About the Author

For twenty-five years, Gloria Dunn has been in the business of helping people in their work environment. She originally developed her skills as a workplace manager and an organizational behavior consultant. Since then, she has gone on to become a professional speaker and provides programs for those who are looking for ways to make their work enrich their lives, and to help organizations improve their people skills and workplace environments. She delivers speeches and offers workshops to groups of all types, including businesses, associations, and the general public. Gloria's speeches are full of wit, wisdom, and practical information that strengthen the will and enrich the spirit and help listeners achieve their loftiest goals. At work, people become more creative and productive, and their morale increases.

As an Aquarius, Gloria is a cross between Albert Schweitzer and Mickey Mouse — that is, a humanitarian and an entertainer. The humanitarian in her wants to help others achieve peace, joy, love, and compassion in life, and to find a deep satisfaction in their work. The Mickey Mouse in her loves to make people smile and get them genuinely interested in going from merely making a living to having a life. Through her company, Wiser Ways to Work®, she is realizing her mission to help humanize the workplace, revitalize the worker, and create organizational harmony.

Index